AMAZING FAITH

STORIES OF
CHRISTIANS
IN DEFINING
MOMENTS

THOMAS A. SHAW
DWIGHT A. CLOUGH

MOODY PUBLISHERS
CHICAGO

© 2003 by
THOMAS A. SHAW AND DWIGHT A. CLOUGH

Library of Congress Cataloging-in-Publication Data

Shaw, Thomas A.
    Amazing faith : amazing faith stories of Christians in defining moments / by
Thomas A. Shaw and Dwight A. Clough.
        p. cm.
    Includes bibliographical references.
    ISBN 0-8024-1358-7
    1. Christian biography. 2. Moody Bible Institute—Alumni and alumnae—
Biography. I. Clough, Dwight A. II. Title.

BR1702 .S53 2003
270.8'2'0922—dc21

2002151840

1 3 5 7 9 10 8 6 4 2

Printed in the United States of America

The encouragement and sacrifice of
our families made this book possible.
Because our families shape us,
they helped to shape the message of this book.
We believe success at home is central,
not peripheral, to Christian ministry.
Therefore, it is our joy to
dedicate *Amazing Faith* to our families.

To my loving wife, Carolyn,
and our children—Andrew, Emily, Catherine, and Robert.
—Thomas A. Shaw

To my wonderful wife, Kim,
and our four precious children—Liza, Hans, Alan, and Sally.
—Dwight A. Clough

CONTENTS

* * *

FOREWORD

* * *

There's nothing like a good story to stir your soul. I grew up hearing my daddy share countless stories about the people who shaped his life and faith—there was the fellow who helped Daddy harness the big draft horses every morning so he could deliver coal, the kindly old woman who taught my father's Sunday school, and the YMCA coach who inspired my dad to try out for the 1932 Olympic wrestling team (and Daddy made it!). It was clear Daddy was standing on the shoulders of these saints; and I, in turn, am standing—or, at least, sitting—on my father's shoulders. All because of the power of people's stories.

This is a book of stories about people of faith. These stories penetrate deep into the heart and soul of humanity, yet convey the character and attributes of God. And as I've learned through the years, when God is involved, nothing is ordinary. In this book you'll discover evidence of the extraordinary work of God—when gloom turned into hope; failure gave way to stunning success; miraculous provision arrived; a medical sentence of death was overturned; and a powerful new life ensued. That's what makes faith so amazing to us. It's really not about us, but God yearning for us to know Him and to glorify Him with our lives. The frailty of humanity energized by God's transforming power. The participants' stories in this book capture that concept.

In reading this book, I couldn't help but relate these stories to a Scripture passage that has been very dear to my own heart:

> We are hard pressed on every side, but not crushed; perplexed, but not in despair; persecuted, but not abandoned; struck down, but not destroyed. We always carry around in our body the death of Jesus, so that the life of Jesus may also be revealed in our body. (2 Corinthians 4:8–10 NIV)

Our heavenly Father uses ordinary people, people just like you and me, to fulfill His purposes. In spite of whatever weaknesses we have, He can work through us. God is our strong rock, a firm defense, and a sure refuge for the weak. But He doesn't always choose to work in the same way in every situation. He releases one person from arrest in the Soviet Union, but brings another home by means of a communist executioner. He allows one person's dream to die, while He multiples the dream of another. He speaks to some on beds of illness, to others as they walk "unprotected" through dangerous inner-city neighborhoods, to others as they are put under pressure to compromise their faith before the leaders of the world.

Everyone has a story. I have a story. You have a story. Be encouraged as you read this book, and know that the same God who proved faithful to these people during defining moments is also with you.

—Joni Eareckson Tada
President, Joni and Friends
Winter 2002

INTRODUCTION

♦   ♦   ♦

THE STORY OF GOD
IN THE LIVES OF HIS PEOPLE

In early 2001, Moody Bible Institute Alumni Association Director Thomas Shaw was thinking, *So many Moody alumni have powerful stories to share. How can we let the world know?*

Meanwhile, 180 miles away, freelance writer Dwight Clough was composing a letter to the Moody Alumni Association:

> *I love a good story. Don't you?*
>
> *In heaven, you'll find me wandering around asking people to tell me the story of what God has done in their lives. I'll eat it up and hang on every word.*

He concluded, "Let's put together a book of testimonies of Moody alumni."

What a coincidence! Two men who had never met were thinking exactly the same thing. Was this God's way of showing us that He wanted His story told in this book?

In the eighteen months that followed, the two of us worked and prayed together with the common goal of telling you the story of what God is doing in the lives of His people and how faithful He is in the defining moments of our lives. God used each of our gifts to make this book come together. While we both interviewed participants and wrote chapters, each of us had a unique role. Tom focused on which stories to tell and arranged interviews, while Dwight helped with a sense of story and with editing the entire manuscript. Except for the two chapters that tell the stories of people who are no longer living, and which are based on biographies, all these stories are based on personal interviews. To make the stories more personal, we've elected to use an "as told to" format, and we have told all the interview stories in the first person.

The sixteen people profiled in this book span a century and have experienced God in almost every kind of situation. One was interrogated by the KGB. Another walked away from a lucrative job with a major TV network. Two were martyred. One was born to former slaves and rose to become an adviser to five U.S. presidents. Another was present when teens drove by shooting with Uzi submachine guns.

Although they all share a common heritage—each is a former Moody student—they are as diverse as you can imagine. Sue Buchanan wanted to use the surplus funds from her women's auxiliary group to buy bathroom scales. George Verwer bartered his wedding cake for gasoline, so that he and his new bride could go to Mexico and spread the Gospel.

Don't be surprised if your world is rocked as you read the stories of these people. Their stories are relevant and powerful. Some of the participants are young, some not as young. But every story is timeless.

They minister in every setting. Some are best-selling authors. Several are involved in strategic racial reconciliation ministry. Others work with satanists and prostitutes in the inner city. Several have carried the Gospel into places hostile to Christianity. One is an Emmy-award-winning journalist.

Every one is a class act. You could call them great men and women of faith. But none of them claims to be a superstar. Instead, each is quick to say, "Apart from Christ, I can do nothing" (see John 15:5).

We are struck with their honesty.

Do you struggle with doubts? So have they. Do you feel as though your prayers go unanswered? If so, read on and discover that you are not alone. Russ Knight tells his story about prayers of faith. Have you ever felt cheated by God? Then don't miss Ruth Senter's powerful struggle with God's goodness.

Have you ever been pressured to compromise your faith? Then read about how Mark Jobe was pressured to cave in when he stood in front of 1,700 business and community leaders at a prestigious university.

Have you ever felt like you don't fit in? Sue Buchanan was told to wash off her "barn paint" (makeup) before she was allowed to play the piano in church. Mary McLeod Bethune was barred from reading, barred from education, and barred from the mission field.

These are men and women of action. When faced with an opportunity, they take it. Ron Hutchcraft chose to take on a new Native American ministry when he and his ministry team were already maxed out. Prolific writer Jerry Jenkins tells of moments when a new Left Behind book needs to be written, a deadline is approaching, and the computer screen is blank.

They have faced every kind of challenge.

What would you do if your fiancé came to you forty-eight hours before your wedding and said, "I haven't been honest with you about something. I've been drinking all along and hiding it from you"?

What would you do if you were given six months to live?

What if you had no food and no money to buy any?

How would your plans for entering college change if you knew a member of your family might die before you returned for Christmas break?

How would you find significance if you slept on a mattress on the floor with a ring of mousetraps around it, listening to gang fights just outside your window?

In this book you'll read about "Psycho," who wanted to blow up the stadium in Denver where the Promise Keepers were meeting. You'll read about being kicked out of countries, about giving up dreams, about being threatened with death, about being accused of building underground missile silos, about being held for ransom.

Two of these people, John and Betty Stam, paid the ultimate price for their faith. They served tea and cake to their captors and were later cut down with the sword. Others are bringing the light of Christ into very dark places. Several learned powerful lessons through serious illness or injury.

Yet you will also read about the creativity of God. God used an unsaved printer to set His plan in motion for a young man needing ministry training. God used a mentally disabled brother to teach a lesson on kindness that led to the salvation of one participant. God used a missionary who never said a word to win a family headed for hell.

These stories focus on defining moments, key events when God showed up and changed the course of someone's life. We want to take you to those times so that we, like they, may come to know God in a deeper, more meaningful way.

Thomas A. Shaw
Dwight A. Clough
August 2002

1

SERVANT OF CHRIST, ADVOCATE FOR EQUALITY

• • •

"Put down that book! *You* can't read!"[1] a little white girl told Mary Jane McLeod during a visit to the neighboring Wilson home. *All* Mary wanted to do was look at a book sitting on the little table. The girl had let Mary play with her dolls, but why did she insult her by not letting her look at the book?

At that moment, Mary began learning what the color of her skin meant in the South in the late 1800s. It made no difference that Mary was bright, eager, and energetic. She was black, and that's all that mattered. Abraham Lincoln's Emancipation Proclamation was more than a decade old, but it would take many more painful decades before it would penetrate the heart of America. Much of white America did not believe that all men were created equal.

Mary yearned to read. As she worked rows of cotton, hoeing out crabgrass on her parents' thirty-acre farm in South Carolina, it was clear to everyone that her mind was elsewhere. She was dreaming of going to school. *White children go to school. Why can't I have what they have?*

Her thirst for learning centered around God and His crea-tion. After the backbreaking work of farming was over, Mary hurried into the cabin to listen to her grandmother tell Bible stories and sing hymns. Mary overwhelmed her grandmother with questions, probing her for more information, so she could understand her family's heritage and her God.

But even though Mary's parents, former slaves Samuel and Patsy McLeod, were God fearing, there was little hope that Mary would ever realize her dream of an education. She would never be admitted to a white school. And schools for black children were few. She and her sixteen siblings would most likely live their lives in oppression and poverty and without any hope for an education.

Still, Mary mustered the courage to ask her father if she could go to school.

"No," he said. Since she was colored, she could not, he explained.

But Mary didn't take no for an answer. She also had a Father in heaven. She turned to Him. Over and over she prayed, *God, make a way for me to get an education.*

The answer came one day as the family was working in a swampy section of their land. Mary's work and prayers were interrupted by a stranger. Miss Emma Wilson came to see them because she was starting a school for black children. This school, financed by the Presbyterian Church, would be set up near their home in Mayesville, South Carolina.

Mary was chosen by her parents and siblings to be the one from their family to attend this new school. However, she couldn't start until the cotton picking was finished. Mary was thrilled—*a miracle had happened!* God had answered her prayers. She was going to school—Mayesville Institute!

Mary prodded her family to work harder and faster than ever that summer to bring in the cotton.

Mary walked five miles to and from school in Mayesville and never missed a day. Her teacher, Miss Wilson, while working with limited educational tools, began teaching the students to read, write, and do arithmetic. Each evening after Mary got home from school, she taught everyone in the family what she had learned. She was a student by day and a teacher by night! As Mary progressed in her reading, she read the Bible to her family. It was as if the Word that they had believed and heard for years now became alive—now that Mary could read to them from the Holy Book.

Mary did well with her studies and was among the first to graduate from Mayesville Institute. Everyone in the community, black and white alike, came to celebrate the accomplishments of these graduates. Though the school only went through the sixth grade, any education for African-Americans in those days was a great step forward.

But the joy of completing her program was suddenly overshadowed with her next roadblock. *How could she go to high school?* It seemed terrible to come this far only to be blocked from progressing further. Mary's father spoke with Miss Wilson about how Mary might continue her education. Miss Wilson knew of a school, Scotia Seminary.

As Mary and her father pondered how Mary might be able to attend Scotia, the family suffered a devastating loss. Their mule died unexpectedly. Without a mule, the ground could not be prepared in time for the upcoming planting season. They had no money or credit left to buy another mule. In a moment of great courage, one of Mary's brothers stepped forward and announced that he would pull the plow. Even though he was very strong, the family knew they must all share in this difficult task—*to be the mule.*

High school would have to wait—maybe for a long time. The proceeds from a good crop the next season would go toward buying a new mule. That left no money for Mary to go to school. Taking her turn at pulling the plow was minor pain in comparison to the thought of not being able to continue her education. Again, Mary pleaded with God to deliver her. *Without school, she had no future.*

God's answer again came through Miss Wilson. She brought the news that a white lady in Colorado, Mary Crissman, wanted to use her modest life savings as a seamstress to educate a black student. Mary, now fifteen years old, could enroll at the Scotia Seminary[2] in Concord, North Carolina. Mary knelt and praised God for providing the funds and delivering her once again. She quickly gathered her belongings and boarded a train to North Carolina to continue her education.

Scotia was a wonderful experience for Mary. For the first time in her life she had both white and black teachers, whom she found to be equally competent, as well as very cordial with each other. Through their example, Mary began to understand the meaning of equality and the realization that she was a first-class, not a second-class citizen. She also began developing other talents, such as singing, public speaking, debating, and drama. She spent a lot of time reading about the history of slavery, which helped her understand the issues and the difficulty America was still struggling to overcome. She also developed a deep desire to serve God on the mission field in Africa. Mary graduated seven years later from Scotia, having taken the "higher course." Dr. Satterfield, the principal, recommended that Mary continue her education at Moody Bible Institute, where she could be trained for missionary service.

Mary's May 26, 1894, letter of application to the registrar at Moody said:

> *It is my greatest desire to enter your Institute for the purpose of receiving Biblical training in order that I may be fully prepared for the great work, which I trust I may be called to do in dark Africa. To be an earnest missionary is the ambition of my life.*
>
> *I was born in Mayesville, South Carolina, July 10th, 1875. My educational advantages were very limited until I came to Scotia Seminary in 1887. I have been here since then and hope to graduate in the Scientific Course here June 13th, '94. My health has been, and is, very good. I shall hope to be able to enter the Institute sometime in July and take the course necessary for my work.*[3]

A few weeks later, Mary was accepted at Moody and on her way to Chicago. What a change the North brought. Mary was met at the train station by a group of Moody students—all of them white! She quickly found out that except for a student from Africa, she was the only black student enrolled that year. She had never experienced being the only black before, because she came from a predominantly black culture. She did find that there were other students who were non-Caucasians in the student body; however, they were Japanese, Chinese, and Indian students. They were very different from each other, but yet they had something in common—they weren't white!

What was it like to be a minority? Mary described it in these words: "White men's eyes piercing me, piercing. Some of them are kind eyes; others would like to be, but are still afraid."[4] Moody had as much to learn about blacks through Mary as Mary had to learn about the Bible and missions from Moody. Yet, in time, Mary felt accepted and a vibrant part of the student body. The school's founder, D. L. Moody, set the tone for race relations at Moody in his interaction with Mary. She described him as a man who had "a love for the whole human family, regardless of creed, class, or color."[5] Late in life, Mary conveyed that her time at MBI was "a very integral part of her education and a very definite force for good in her life's work."[6]

Mary was a doer. She realized that she needed not just Bible knowledge but also ministry experience to prepare her for a career as a missionary. Mary threw herself into field-work with a passion. She went door-to-door evangelizing, sang to prisoners at the police station, and served meals at Pacific Garden Mission. She met with success as an evangelist.[7] Mary's wonderful mezzo-soprano voice captivated audiences of all sizes. As a member of the Gospel Choir team, she traveled for the school performing concerts in churches.

After a year at Moody, in June 1895, Mary made her way to New York to seek approval from the Presbyterian Board for Missions to be one of their missionaries in Africa.

The board did not approve her appointment. *There are no openings for a Negro in Africa at this time.*

Mary was shocked and disappointed. *Perhaps they will approve me later,* she thought.

Instead of sitting still, Mary found another opportunity to serve the Lord. Through the Presbyterian Board of Education she obtained a teaching job at the Haines Normal Institute in Augusta, Georgia.

At Haines, Mary found a mentor in the person of Lucy

Laney, who founded the school a few years earlier. She was twenty years older than Mary but shared a similar past. She too came from a very poor black family and rose out of that poverty because of her thirst for knowledge. Lucy helped Mary come to closure about not being accepted to be a missionary to Africa. Lucy explained that Africans in America needed the Lord just as much as those in Africa. Mary began to understand the importance of educating black Americans. Entering the depressed areas of Augusta, she brought thousands of children to Haines to teach them the Bible and to sing hymns. Every day, she sent them home with tracts to share with their families.

It soon became clear to Mary that she had found her calling. She was serving God by educating young black children in the South.

After a year at Haines, the Presbyterian Board gave Mary a new teaching assignment. She was sent to the Kindell Institute, another church-supported school for blacks in Sumter, North Carolina. During her years at Kindell, Mary kept very little from her paychecks, sending most of her money to her family to pay off the mortgage on the house and to put two of her sisters through Scotia.

While in Sumter, Mary met, and later married, Albertus Bethune in 1898. Soon after their marriage, they moved to Savannah, Georgia, where Albertus had a teaching position. Mary sought a teaching job to supplement their income but soon gave up that idea. After their baby, Albert McLeod Bethune, was born, Mary stayed at home caring for him. During that time, Mary's concern for her son and for thousands like him coalesced into a dream.

"I'd been dreaming," she later said, "all my life, down yonder in the cotton fields, in the classroom, singing in the

Chicago slums, dreaming, dreaming of big buildings and little children—my *own* institution."[8]

She determined to start her school in a place where black children had no opportunity for an education. Consumed by this dream, she persuaded Albertus to let her go with the baby to Palatka, Florida, to scout out areas in need of a school. Albertus reluctantly agreed, assuming that the difficulties she encountered would discourage her and they would return to Savannah. He was wrong! While Mary was searching, she held a teaching position at Palatka Mission School. The school was energized by her presence. The letters Mary wrote to Albertus were filled with great excitement for what the Lord was doing there. He realized it was no use. He left Savannah and moved to Palatka. It was obvious Mary was on a mission and was not coming back to Georgia.

During her quest to find a place for a school, Mary visited points along the Atlantic coastline of Florida from Miami in the south to Flagler in the north. A lot of construction was taking place along the coastline, and the developers preferred using black labor because it was cheaper. When she came to Daytona Beach, her heart was moved with compassion for the poor conditions the blacks had to endure in the midst of a beautiful area with palmetto and evergreen oak trees. This was it! This was the city that needed a school for black children.

Mary found temporary housing in Daytona Beach with some old friends and began searching for a home. With only one dollar and fifty cents, she convinced a landlord to rent her a simple cottage on 529 Oak Street for eleven dollars a month. Mary used four tiny rooms on the first floor for a school while her family lived in the three rooms upstairs. Within a month of her arrival in Daytona, she had opened her school—the Daytona Educational and Industrial Training School for Negro Girls. She started with five girls and one boy, her son Albert. The parents of the girls paid fifty cents a week for tuition. Things were extremely tight financially as they scraped together enough to operate. They were creative: "Pupils used homemade elderberry juice for ink and wrote with quills they fashioned themselves."[9] Mary and her friends searched the refuse piles for salvageable items to sell. Mary also asked the community for donations of unwanted items. Throughout the struggles of those early years, Mary stated, "Mama, Papa, Dr. Satterfield, Dwight Moody, Lucy Laney, I haven't forgotten any of you! Your training hasn't been wasted."[10]

Mary inspired her students. Parents and visitors often came to watch her lead the students in prayer and deliver speeches casting a vision of what these young people could become. Academic subjects and practical training were delivered in a context of Christian education and devotion to Christ.

How did a struggling school for black students survive and grow in the early 1900s? The Lord gave Mary the plan. Using an idea she borrowed from Fisk University's Jubilee Singers, she organized her students into a ministry team that went into the community to sing before groups of people. Because Daytona Beach was a developing resort area, wealthy vacationers, such as John D. Rockefeller, James N. Gamble of Proctor & Gamble, Thomas H. White of White Sewing Machine Company, and Andrew Carnegie visited the community. These and others became acquainted with Mary's school and provided resources to keep the struggling school afloat.

Again, Albertus was one step behind Mary. He was back in Palatka wondering where their next move would be. From the tone in Mary's letters, he knew that even though the work in Daytona Beach was a struggle, it was advancing under Mary's leadership. So, he joined his wife and son in Daytona, where he began driving a taxi.

Within two years Mary was educating two hundred and fifty students, using volunteer and paid teachers. They quickly outgrew their first facility and rented a building next door until Mary could find a more permanent location. The school was eventually located on a city dump known as "Hell's Hole." Mary saw potential in this property on Second Avenue and persuaded the owner to sell it for two hundred dollars. Mary didn't have the five-dollar down payment but quickly earned it—selling ice cream and sweet-potato pies to construction workers by the beach.

Growth and construction created more fund-raising challenges. Many times the school was only days from closure. Mary was determined to build this school. The children were worth it! But a building project takes a lot of money, and at first progress was slow. Mary later reported:

> One of my most important jobs was to be a good beggar! I rang doorbells and tackled cold prospects without a lead. I wrote articles for whoever would print them, distributed leaflets, rode interminable miles of dusty roads on my old bicycle, invaded churches, clubs, lodges, chambers of commerce. If a prospect refused to make a contribution, I would say, "thank you for your time." No matter how deep my hurt, I always smiled. I refused to be discouraged, for neither God nor man can use a discouraged person.[11]

Finally, Thomas H. White, the owner of the White Sewing Machine Company, provided a large sum for this project capital, but also left a trust fund of $67,000, from which the school could use the interest for ongoing expenses. The building was finished and dedicated in 1907. White cared deeply for Mary's school and her students. He knew that anything he gave to the school would be greatly appreciated and wisely used. He often stopped by unannounced and dropped off shoes and blankets for needy students. His generosity was duplicated hundreds of times over as people heard about the school and made contributions to help develop its campus and to provide for everyday needs.

A year later, Mary changed the name of the school and began enrolling male students.

About that time, Booker T. Washington, founder of the Tuskegee Institute, visited the school. Kindred spirits, Mary and Dr. Washington dreamed together of a day when blacks and whites could get along, a day when opportunities would be open to all races to pursue the American dream. Her dream was expressed in her simple prayer: *Dear Lord, help my people! Help me to help my people!*[12] Dr. Washington was impressed with Mary and saw to it that others with influence around the country knew about her school.

Mary's dream was becoming a reality. Black students were learning, graduating, and making a better life for themselves. Outreach programs in the community were bringing races together in a time of worship to God. Every Sunday afternoon at three o'clock in Faith Hall, interracial services were held. The meetings grew so popular that latecomers had to stand outside and listen. The music, poetry, and sermons inspired all who came to worship God.

There was a price to be paid for all this progress. That price turned out to be her marriage. While she invested her energy into the development of her school, Mary and

Albertus drifted apart. They decided to permanently separate in 1908, after ten years of marriage. Albertus moved back to the Carolinas, while Mary raised their son in Daytona Beach.

♦   ♦   ♦

The school Mary founded later became Bethune-Cookman College. But her influence spread far beyond her school. She was invited to serve with the National Association of Colored Women, National Association for the Advancement of Colored People, the National Council of Negro Women, the National Urban League, and the Association for the Study of Negro Life and History.

Viewed by blacks and whites as a diplomatic link between the two races, Mary served on two president-appointed committees. She served as special assistant to the secretary of war for the selection of candidates for first officer status during World War II. She became the first black woman in American history to head a federal agency when she became the director of the Division of Negro Affairs of the National Youth Administration. She represented President Truman for the inauguration ceremonies in Liberia in 1952.

Mary became a friend of Eleanor Roosevelt. Mary and the first lady shared the stage on many occasions to advance the rights of blacks in America.

Mary has been described as "undoubtedly the most influential and famous black female in American education and politics during the first half of the twentieth century."[13]

In 1985 a U.S. postage stamp was issued in her honor as a part of the Black Heritage stamp series. Additionally, she received eleven honorary degrees and advised five U.S. presidents on black affairs and education.

Throughout her life, the oppression of African-Americans was real, but Mary did not let it hold her back. Rather, it inspired her to turn the tide of racism in the United States. Relying on her heavenly Father for ability, strength, endurance, provision, and wisdom, she strove to make a difference for the rights of her people. God had gifted her with a sharp mind to maneuver throughout society to educate not only African-Americans, but also those who held illogical and ungodly prejudices.

In spite of the obstacles that stood before her, Mary McLeod Bethune demonstrated *amazing faith*. She was a servant of Christ and an advocate for equality.

◆   ◆   ◆

Mary McLeod Bethune was born in 1875. She spent her final years in Daytona Beach until a heart attack took her life on May 18, 1955. She attended Moody's Undergraduate School 1894–95.

2

A WHOLE
NEW BEGINNING

◆　　◆　　◆

THE STORY OF
SUE DAVIS BUCHANAN

"Your mother is as good as dead."

My daughter's friend was talking about me. Coming from a physician's family, she knew the medical truth: Nobody expected me to survive.

It happened like this: I complained of pain. "Don't worry," the doctor said. "There's no pain with breast cancer . . . unless, of course, it's in the latter stages."

I went back to work and tried not to worry. I tried to think about my work. I was trying to focus on the client in my office when my secretary interrupted. I had a phone call. "It's your doctor," my secretary apologized. "He says it's urgent."

I picked up the phone. "We need a biopsy," the doctor said. "I wouldn't wait if I were you."

When I arrived at his office, the doctor had papers for me to sign. "Probably nothing," he said, "but if we do get in there and find a problem, we'll need to take the breast."

Things were moving too fast. *I thought this was a biopsy.* I didn't want to go to sleep and wake up without a breast. I wrote "LUMPECTOMY ONLY!!!" with a Magic Marker across my chart, but it was no use. My life was already on an out-of-control flight I didn't schedule. I was on a journey I didn't want to take.

A mastectomy followed, and then twelve months of chemotherapy, bringing with it everything from hair loss to hallucinations, from nausea to night terrors.

The night terrors were the worst. Again and again they came back, sometimes more than once a night. Often I fell asleep at my normal time only to wake minutes later in panic. My body, drenched in sweat, tossed as my mind careened through all my fears. *Will I go through the misery of chemotherapy only to find out it hasn't done its job? Will I die? Will I be a bedridden burden to my family? Will I see my oldest daughter graduate from college and my youngest from high school? Will I be around for their weddings? Will I know my grandchildren?*

I felt my prayers were not working. I couldn't find any prayer words. When I tried, the words fell flat, bouncing off the ceiling fan, coming back in my face to mock me. Sometimes I got angry. Sometimes I yelled and screamed at God, "Are You there? Are You listening? Where are You?"

It wasn't as though God and I were strangers. My parents were Christians; with all their might they were Christians. They took me to a Bible church where the Sunday school teachers pounded Scripture into us. Learning Bible verses was serious business when I was a kid. In our church they did everything to make sure we could quote as many of them as possible. They tricked us. They bribed us. They cajoled us. They bombarded us with Scripture.

But even though I embraced the faith of my parents and my church, I never really fit in. When I was supposed to be listening to the sermon, I was thinking about throwing spit-balls at the bald man in the second row. Even as a young child, I had my own unique identity.

In my neighborhood, I was Mrs. Vandertweezers, dressed in mama's cast-off satin blouse that dragged the floor on me, high-heeled shoes, a big hat with a veil, plenty of glittery jewelry, gobs of makeup, and—for a final touch around the neck—an animal that bit its own tail. Down the street past the convent I strolled, pushing my baby buggy. Inside, my cat, Smokey the Pirate Don Derek of Don Day, squirmed in doll clothes. I greeted the neighbors and brought them up to date on the activities of "Manny," my imaginary husband.

When I returned from these walks, Mother often looked at Daddy and said, "She's not like my family." He shook his head. "She's not like our family." Then Mother looked at me and said, "Children should be seen and not heard. Especially you, honey."

I grew up, not a rebel, but not exactly a soldier in uniform. Even though I grew older, the Mrs. Vandertweezers persona never really left me. I wore makeup, though it was against the rules in my very conservative church. (When they were short a pianist, they asked me to go to the restroom, wash off my "barn paint," and return to the platform so I could "serve the Lord.") I went to Kings College and Moody Bible Institute for all the wrong reasons—to kiss and be kissed. College leaders met with me privately to see if there was some way I could disguise my Dolly Parton figure.

I got married, but I didn't settle down the way church people wanted me to. I was asked to join a women's auxiliary at a Bible college. I jumped in and suggested they use their budget surplus to buy bathroom scales. "The women in the dorms are getting fat," I explained. "We need something so they can weigh themselves."

Horror filled their faces. Finally, the director spoke: "Don't you realize this is the Lord's money? Don't you realize there are retired missionaries who can't afford proper underwear?"

So we bought underwear. The missionary sent it back (five times), but we bought underwear.

◆　　◆　　◆

And now, I had cancer. My hair fell out. I wore an artificial breast. And I was very, very sick.

The day after my mastectomy, a beautiful woman walked into my hospital room. "I came to encourage you," she said. "I came to tell you that having cancer was the greatest privilege of my life."

I wanted to slap her.

How could having cancer be a privilege? Doesn't she know that Daddy died of cancer? Doesn't she know that Mother has been fighting a losing battle with cancer? Hasn't she heard that my three best girlfriends from high school are all dead, each one lost to breast cancer?

Her words, though unwelcome at the time, stayed with me, and they proved to be prophetic.

◆　　◆　　◆

My life before cancer is a dream with soft edges and blurred images. That dream ended the day I awoke with breast cancer. I say that I *awoke* at age forty-five with breast cancer. In a very real sense, that is true. In my struggle against this disease, I awoke in stages, to a God I didn't realize was there, to a place of belonging I never had before, and to a new identity and mission in life.

I never expected Scripture to come alive to me like it did during that year. Before cancer, the many verses I had memorized as a child were to me mere platitudes, nice sayings, "out there" someplace, not having much to do with me. But as I lay in that hospital bed, passages that had been ribbons and awards at Bible memory meets suddenly exploded with meaning.

Oh! Ohh! I was startled by the impact of it all. *This is what the Bible means when it speaks of the "peace that passes understanding."*

Scripture sustained me. It encouraged me. It empowered me. It got me through that horrible year. When I couldn't pray, I prayed Scriptures. Scripture enabled me to answer the "Why me?" Scripture helped me face the fact that I truly might die.

"For to me, to live is Christ, and to die is gain" became more than just the saying of an ancient apostle. It was transformed to gut-level truth.

◆   ◆   ◆

Possibly because I didn't fit in the church of my childhood, to me God was incredibly complicated. He had expectations I wasn't sure I wanted to face. *What if He didn't like me as the grown-up Mrs. Vandertweezers?* I didn't want to get into trouble. But I didn't want to push my luck either, by getting too inquisitive about divine requirements. *After all, truly spiritual people are missionaries who never wear makeup, aren't they?*

But the God who met me in my time of greatest need was not complicated or unreasonable. He didn't care if I wore makeup and jewelry, how I fixed my hair, or whether I tried to disguise my figure. None of those things mattered to Him.

The God who met me showed me that He was as close as I wanted Him to be. That little signs of His presence were all around me. That He only wanted one thing from me: He wanted me to be His person.

God's will for my life is not some great unfathomable mystery. It's really quite simple. All I need do is be His person one day at a time. Available. Open to His Spirit.

◆　　　◆　　　◆

With the realization that I am accepted by God for who I am came the wonderful freedom to be part of the community of Christians. In the place of those who wanted me to wash off my "barn paint" and disguise my figure, God brought friends into my life who embraced me for who I am —a high-energy, quirky personality with all the trappings of a party girl.

When I faced great challenge, these friends were there for me.

When the night terrors got so bad that even prescription drugs wouldn't take them away, a friend came up to me and told me her experience with cancer and with those same nighttime fears. "I didn't want to live, it was so bad," she said. "But a friend of mine came to me and said, 'June, I'm going to pray for you. I'm going to ask God to take away your fear. I won't stop praying till He answers.' Sue, I can tell you the minute and the hour my fear went away! I felt free and I knew it was gone!"

She paused, then leaned forward and touched me. "Sue, am I supposed to be that person in your life? The person who prays till the fear stops?"

There are some loads we cannot carry alone. I accepted her offer. I let go of my pills and trusted God to answer her prayers. When I did, I slept like a baby, and the terrors never returned.

Another friend, Joy MacKenzie, made me a promise. "If you stay alive, if you make it through chemotherapy, I will take you to the Cayman Islands." She was good on her word. As soon as chemo was finished—I was still a little woozy—she bought tickets, and we flew to Grand Cayman.

That trip was the repair shop that restored my ability to focus.

Before my mastectomy, year of chemotherapy, and reconstructive surgery, I wasn't the world's most caring, nurturing, do-unto-others, love-your-neighbor-as-yourself kind of person (although I would feed someone's cat if asked). But during this struggle, I began to find a new empathy that I had never felt before. For cancer patients, of course. But also for angry doctors who secretly carry a heavy load of accountability for a patient's life. For nurses who cry at night for patients they've lost. For hospital visitors who pray a loud prayer and pronounce you healed—whether you are or aren't—and sincerely believe they have given you a gift. And for anyone struggling, whether a mother with a disabled child or a teen who has lost her way.

I started keeping a journal. Only cancer could have caused me to do that. My last experience with writing had been in high school when the teacher waved my work in front of the class as an example of how *not* to write. Though certain I was no writer, I wrote because I didn't know if I would survive. I wanted my daughters to have something in their hands that would preserve my last days for them.

Several years after the breast cancer, a good friend said, "You know, we ought to tell your story. I often ghostwrite stories. Your story would give many people hope." The friend was Jerry Jenkins, who went on to coauthor the Left Behind series.

"Oh, I hate to show you my journal," I told him. "I've never written anything."

"Let me see it," he encouraged. Then he looked at it and said, "You need an agent." Shortly thereafter, he introduced me to one.

The result was my first book, *I'm Alive and the Doctor's Dead.* The book was a success, but I was certain that was a fluke. Yet, I've written other books, some by myself and some with Gloria Gaither, and they've all been successful. Then came award-winning children's books and a humorous line of greeting cards about dysfunction, hot flashes, chemotherapy, and—yes!—throwing spitballs in church.

The books put me out there as a speaker, first to secular audiences. I could not have chosen that role. I never looked at a speaker and said, "Oh, I'd like to be a speaker." I'd sooner be an astronaut than a speaker. But there I was, following speakers such as Joan Lunden. And then I began to get calls about speaking to Christians. I said, "No, no, no, no, no, no, no. I can't do that. There are so many good Christian speakers."

God, I prayed, *I just don't want to do this. I'm not very good at it.*

I felt as though the Lord said to me in my spirit, *Well, if you were going to do one thing for the rest of your life, what would it be?*

I wondered, *What would I like to do? I'd like to make peo-*

ple laugh. People carry such heavy burdens, so just for a few minutes I'd like to help them get their minds off their burdens and let them laugh.

Then that little voice said, *You have the opportunity to do just that!*

From that point on, I've spoken to both the secular and the Christian world. Everywhere I go, I share what God has taught me about reclaiming our lives, our future, and our faith after a crisis.

God doesn't need me to write or speak or talk to people on planes about Him, but He sure wants me to. He wants me to be His person, His representative. And I know that I'm not qualified for anything, except as His person. As time has gone on, it has become easy for me to share my faith with people.

I once visited Davis, California, the self-proclaimed most liberal community in the United States. Everyone there is highly intellectual—off the chart. The town's four bookstores contain all the books you might want about goddesses and magic.

I stopped in a store and met some adorable young women. We hit it off right away. One of them told me about some oil you can hold in your hand and find spiritual energy. One girl—probably the funkiest of all with a big tattoo on her back, dressed in black with black spiked hair, and lots of piercings, but cute as a bug—asked me what I spoke about.

I said, "I speak about reclaiming your life after a crisis."

"Tell me about it," she said. "I have been there." Then she asked, "What do you tell them?"

I said, "I talk to people about reclaiming their lives in increments. You reclaim your health, your sense of humor, your family, your friends, and your faith."

And then I stopped.

She said, "Faith? I've never had a faith. I've *never* had a faith. Just recently I decided because I have a little child, I need to have a faith. You'll never believe it—I can barely bring this out of my mouth—I went to a Baptist church two weeks ago."

I smiled and said, "Oh, I am so excited for you! God is pursuing you. The fact that I am here this very minute and have come into your life, tells me that you are on the right path, and He wants to know you and He wants you to know Him. It's the greatest adventure of your life!"

She got excited because I was excited. As a result, I was able to talk to her a little bit about the truth and where to find truth. I said, "You are so funky—and so off the charts—and I am too. I have a copy of Scripture called *The Message.* I'm going to send it to you, and I'm going to send you a couple other things—and my children's book, *I Love You This Much,* for your little boy."

So I sent her a package. In that package were true stories about people who had come to know the Lord from different places, and I sent her a book with a note: "This will show you exactly, step by step, how to find Him." I wrote a prayer for her that she would come to know Jesus.

This is the epiphany that came to me when I thought I was dying: All God wants is for me to be His person. On that particular day, being His person meant talking to that darling young tattooed, pierced girl, and later sending her what God laid on my heart to send.

◆　　　◆　　　◆

One day, I was driving home from work after a rainstorm when the sun was coming out. I looked up and saw a double rainbow. Even though I was driving on the expressway, even though it was rush hour, I pulled over to the side just to sit there and look at it. Something made me look back, and there, behind me, was a whole line of cars that had pulled over to do just what I was doing.

I wonder what they've been through, I asked myself. *Have they had cancer? What tuned them in to the little signals of God's presence and care?*

◆   ◆   ◆

My mind drifts back to Daddy's final days. Even though he had a year of dreadful suffering, his last day on earth was a bright and shining moment in my memory. The sun streamed through the windows of the back bedroom where he lay racked with pain, weighing less than sixty-five pounds. His last words to me were: "It's so beautiful!" His eyes were shut, so I knew he was seeing something I couldn't see.

I left the room and walked to the kitchen door. I gazed out, looking upward at the steep hill immediately behind the house. A light rain now took the place of the sunshine. Before me was a mysterious path of yellow rose petals stretching up the slope as far as I could see. *This is strange,* I thought. *There are no rosebushes nearby. Where did this come from?* I opened the screen door and stepped out onto the porch. The fragrance of roses was overwhelming, as was the peace that blanketed my spirit.

When I returned Daddy was gone. But his last words remain with me: "It's so beautiful!"

I close my eyes as well, and I realize that the party isn't here. The real party is somewhere else.

◆   ◆   ◆

Twenty years after her experience of cancer, **Sue Buchanan**
(Undergraduate School 1957–58) continues to bring hope,
humor, and encouragement to people in crisis through her books
and her speaking engagements. She and her husband, Wayne
(former director of Moody Bible Institute's Correspondence
School), make their home in Nashville, Tennessee. You may
learn more about her and her ministry through her Website,
www.suebue.com.

3

LOVE SPEAKS
EVERY LANGUAGE

◆ ◆ ◆

| THE STORY OF
GARY CHAPMAN |

Our answer is no.

I read the letter one more time. I couldn't believe it. After ten years of preparing to go to the mission field, we were being turned down. The mission board said no.

They're making a huge mistake, I thought. *Don't they realize that God has called us to the mission field? How can they do this to us? At their request, I spent two years of my life as a pastor. They said I needed the experience. When I told them I wanted to teach foreign nationals, they talked me into spending three more years getting a doctorate. How can they do this?*

I reread their reason. They said my wife wouldn't make it on the mission field. They said her health was a problem.

It's a problem, but it's not that big of a problem. Ulcers, illnesses, back problems—everybody has health challenges. It isn't as though we haven't lived with this!

"Physically, Karolyn won't make it," they told me.

My thoughts turned from the mission board to God. *What are You doing, Lord? What is going on? I thought You called me to be a missionary. Why is this door slamming shut? How could You let this mission board reject us?*

I felt as if our compass had been taken away. We had no direction, no plan. *What are we going to do now? We've spent ten years getting ready for the mission field. What are we going to do now?*

◆　　◆　　◆

The logic of missions first gripped me when I was a student at Moody Bible Institute. About 95 percent of Christian workers are working in America, yet 95 percent of the world's population lives somewhere else. That made no sense. I wanted to help end the disparity.[1]

By the time I was a senior, I was president of the campus missionary union. I was also certain that God had called me to be a missionary. When I went on to Wheaton College to finish my degree,[2] I chose anthropology as my major, because I wanted to learn how to minister across cultures.

But something happened that I didn't expect. When I began to study anthropology and philosophy, an unsettling realization crept in: Not everybody believes what I believe. I started asking hard questions about my Christian faith. *Is this really true? Or do I believe this simply because I grew up this way?* Doubts crowded my mind. *What if it isn't true? What if it's all a myth?*

I had to find out. Because the University of Chicago was nearby, I went there to listen to lectures by others who looked at matters of faith differently than I had. I wanted to be open to the truth.

One day I went to a lecture by a liberal theologian. He propounded the idea that Jesus was the illegitimate son of

Mary and a Roman soldier. After listening to his talk, I walked on the streets of Chicago and said to myself, *If what that guy says is true, then there is absolutely no meaning to life. It makes no sense at all.* I felt despair. *I would hate to believe what he believes. I don't think I could live, believing what he believes.*

In this context, I read about the experience of Billy Graham. He had doubts. For a while, he questioned God and the authority of Scripture. After struggling with these doubts, he finally said to God, "I believe. I don't have all the answers, but I want You to know that I believe. And I'm trusting You to give me the answers I need."

I can do that, I said to myself. I realized that there is a difference between doubt and unbelief. Doubt was OK, but unbelief was sin. I chose to believe with my doubts, rather than be an unbeliever with my doubts. I realized then that belief was a choice—based on evidence—but not requiring *all* the evidence. I spoke to God. "I don't have all the answers, and I'm still struggling with a lot of things, but I want You to know that I choose to believe and I give my life to You again in a fresh way."

That moment was like coming home from a journey in the wilderness. That decision turned the course of my journey back to God, and away from unbelief.

◆   ◆   ◆

God brought me through that storm and then taught me another valuable lesson that has stayed with me all my life. After graduating from Wheaton College, I went to Colorado Springs to work with the Navigators for three months in their summer training program. In addition to training, conferences, discipleship groups, and Bible study, the Navigators assigned each person to a forty-hour-a-week job.

My job was to operate a six-foot-long Baum Folder, a machine that took a sheet of paper a yard square and folded it into a pamphlet four inches by six inches.

Simple.

"The key to the whole process," my trainer explained to me, "is getting the right pressure on the rollers. If you don't, the folds are crooked, and by the time it gets to the other end, everything is super crooked and unusable."

No problem, I thought. *I'm a college graduate. I can do whatever needs to be done. Just give me a little instruction, and I can handle it. I can handle anything.*

He gave me a little instruction. Then he walked away.

I began to try to make it all work, and it didn't work.

A couple hours later, he came back and gave me more instruction.

I've got it this time, I thought. He left. I couldn't make it work.

He came back. He showed me again. It looked simple. He left. I tried it. It didn't work.

This went on all day.

Day two was a repeat of day one. Same with day three. I tried and failed, tried and failed, tried and failed every day for a whole week. I never produced anything. I just couldn't get it working. Every day he came by three or four times, spent an hour with me, and tried to help me learn the process.

Then it went on every day for a second week. *Two weeks!* I was two weeks into this, and I still hadn't produced *anything.*

What am I doing here? I asked myself. I was ready to kick the machine, and my self-confidence was at a new low.

After two weeks, early on a Sunday morning, I sat, Bible

in hand, on a huge stone in the middle of the dry moat that encircled the Navigator headquarters, and tried to figure this out. I started reading John, chapter 15. When I read verse 5, the words jumped off the page. Jesus said, "Without Me you can do nothing."

I suddenly understood the lesson of the folding machine. God was teaching me something I needed for life.

Tears filled my eyes as I prayed, *Lord, I agree. I can't run this folder. I cannot do it. I've been trying for two weeks. I can't do it. And I want to acknowledge to You that I can't do anything.*

For the next thirty minutes, I went through my whole life, acknowledging to God that I couldn't do anything anywhere—any kind of work, whether spiritual, mechanical, or anything else—without Him.

At the conclusion of all that confession, that admission to God that He was right, I prayed, *Lord, please give me the ability to do what You want me to do in life, because I can't do anything. Right now, I need the ability to run this folding machine, so I'm asking You to give me that ability.*

That was Sunday morning. Monday morning I went to work. I did the same thing I had been doing for two weeks, and it worked! I didn't have any more trouble the rest of the summer.

◆　　　◆　　　◆

Not long after this, Karolyn and I were married. Like most young couples, we had many struggles in the early days of our marriage. As I prayed through these challenges, again God brought back to me the lesson of the folding machine. *I can't make this work,* I told the Lord. *I've tried everything I know to try, and our marriage is not getting any better. And I don't know what else to do. And I'm asking You to show me what to do.* When David inquired of the Lord to know how to engage the Philistines, God gave him a strategy (2 Samuel 5:22–25). In the same way, God gave me a strategy.

God spoke to me. Although I didn't hear an audible voice, I heard it as clearly as anything I've ever heard.

Why don't you read the life of Jesus?

I was incredulous. *Read the life of Jesus? I'm in seminary now. I've been through Moody. I've read the life of Jesus many times.*

I heard it again. *Why don't you read the life of Jesus?*

OK, I'll read it, I agreed. *If I've missed anything, please show me.*

♦   ♦   ♦

I read Matthew, Mark, Luke, and John looking for the secret to marriage that I had missed. I found it in John 13. Jesus washed the feet of His disciples. When I read that, I realized that I had gone about my marriage in exactly the opposite way of what the Bible prescribes. I had the attitude of, *Look, Karolyn, just listen to me, let me tell you how it works, and everything will be fine.* When I reread John 13, I realized that my job was not to boss her around; my job was to serve her.

That's when I began to ask God to give me the ability to serve her. That's when I began to ask her, "What can I do for you? How can I make your life easier? How can I be a better husband?" When I began to ask those questions and let her teach me how to serve her, our marriage began to get better.

◆   ◆   ◆

These were powerful lessons—lessons I was sure would make us much more effective on the mission field.

But now, the mission board had turned us down. And I couldn't understand how the mission board could make such a terrible mistake.

I wrestled with their decision until one day a friend gently asked, "Gary, could it not be that God is using the mission board to show you His plan for your life?"

You mean God is showing me His will through the mission board's decision?

That was a brand-new idea to me. But it made me think. *If God truly is sovereign, then ultimately man cannot thwart God's plan for my life. Maybe He is using the mission board to give me some direction that I haven't thought about yet. Maybe He's showing me that He can speak through other people, that He not only speaks to the individual, but He can also speak through the community.*

Slowly I absorbed this new reality. *God is redirecting me. But to what? What does He want me to do?*

As I puzzled over that, I considered my passion for teaching. *If God doesn't want me to teach overseas,* I thought, *maybe He wants me to teach here. That way I can prepare missionaries to go overseas.*

Armed with a new objective, I polished my résumé and sent it out to twenty-seven colleges.

No response. No offers. Just rejection letters.

OK, God, what next?

About this time, a friend called us. "How would you like to move from Texas to North Carolina to work as a youth minister for three months?" he asked.

"Well," I answered, "I don't have anything else to do."

♦   ♦   ♦

Compared to our plans to go to the mission field, a summer job as a youth pastor could have seemed almost trivial. But God used it to unfold His plan for us. When summer ended, I fell into a position as a teacher at a small Bible college. I taught there for three years and made another discovery. I love teaching, but I don't like tests, grades, and the whole academic setting. God had a different plan for me. He wanted me to teach, but in a church setting. In 1971 I joined the staff of Calvary Baptist Church, and I've been on staff with Calvary ever since.

As a pastor on staff at this church, I started working in college ministry. We started with four people, and God grew it to three hundred. As we worked with college students, it soon became clear that marriage was a hot topic. Every year I taught a three-month class on preparation for marriage. This class drew more interest and more people than any other. My first book, *Toward a Growing Marriage,* grew out of the work I did with this class.

Then, in 1977, our senior pastor asked me to start a single-adult ministry. In those days few churches were reaching out to separated, divorced, and single adults.

Overnight it exploded. We went from nothing to three hundred single adults almost overnight. I discovered that people who had never cared about God or spiritual things came to church looking for answers when their marriage broke down. I looked for ways to bring God's healing into these lives and marriages, and the result was my second book, *Hope for the Separated.*

After seven years, my ministry focus changed to married adults. Years earlier these married adults had learned about our three-month marriage course for college students and asked, "Why don't you do something for us?" I started developing workshops and classes for married couples, and, eventually, that became the focus of my ministry.

After a while, other churches began to ask me to offer marriage enrichment courses. Those invitations grew into a conference ministry.

In the process of teaching all these courses, many people came to me and asked to talk with me privately about their marriages. In these counseling settings, a picture emerged. Many couples were not able to resolve conflict because neither spouse felt loved. Both felt empty. As a result, these marriages had deteriorated into battlefields, with neither spouse able to win.

I looked for answers, and I quickly realized that what made one spouse feel loved did not necessarily make the other spouse feel loved. When it came to love, each spouse seemed to be speaking a different language. While one marriage partner tried to express love by giving gifts, the other partner longed for touch and physical closeness. In another marriage, one spouse tried to say "I love you" with acts of service, while the other was begging for words of affirmation.

About 1987 I presented a lecture in which I described five "love languages" and encouraged married people to identify and speak their partner's "love language." The response was overwhelming. People connected with the idea. When couples started speaking each other's love language, the whole emotional climate of the marriages changed. Emptiness gave way to a feeling of being loved. Long-standing conflicts were resolved. Marriages were back on track.

After giving this lecture a number of times and getting the same response, the idea for a book was born. Before I wrote it, I went through my counseling notes collected over twenty years. When people said, "I feel like my spouse doesn't love me," what did they want? I tabulated the results, and these same five love languages emerged. From that research, I wrote the 1992 book, *The Five Love Languages*.

At the time I wrote the book, I never thought it would be used in other cultures. Having majored in anthropology, I was sensitive to cultures, and I was really writing for the Western world. That's all I had in mind. I was surprised when foreign publishers started picking up on it. It became a best-seller not only in English, but also in French, in German, in Spanish. In total, it has been published in more than thirty languages. The book has circled the globe.

I had no idea that the principles God showed me in those counseling sessions were universal. The five love languages are spoken the world over. They may be applied somewhat differently from culture to culture, but the fundamental languages seem to be common to all humanity.

That was both a surprise and an encouragement.

One day, we were unwrapping the author's copies of a new foreign language edition, when Karolyn looked at me and said, "You realize what God is doing, don't you?"

"What are you talking about?" I asked.

She answered, "You know how much we wanted to go to the mission field. God is now doing what we wanted to do. God is doing it His way. You are a missionary. Your books have gone all over the world in your place."

It wasn't until that moment that it dawned on me that God really had answered our prayers. We were missionaries.

We held each other and wept.

◆   ◆   ◆

God's plans are always better than our plans. His vision is higher and greater than ours. We struggled with that mission board's decision. Yet, in retrospect, we see the wisdom of it. Karolyn's health would have suffered on the foreign mission field, whereas she has done well here in the States. I am much happier teaching in church and conference settings than I would have been teaching at a seminary, even a seminary for foreign nationals. Although there is nothing wrong with working in one place, reaching one people, God, in His providence, opened the door for us to reach people of many cultures.

Sometimes roadblocks are not roadblocks; they are a direction signal from God.

◆   ◆   ◆

God led me into the realization that marriage and family are not peripheral; they are central under the lordship of Christ. My ministry to my wife is my most important ministry. If I don't get ministry right within my family, all my other ministries will suffer. If I make my family the priority that it should be, then all my other ministries will flow out of experiencing a real walk with God in the context of my own home.

In the past, many Christian leaders have ignored this reality. By doing so, at times the church has been part of the problem, rather than part of the solution. But now the church is rediscovering the importance of the home. Families are being reconciled; marriages are being healed.

As long as the Lord gives me breath, I want to be part of that healing process.

◆   ◆   ◆

Dr. Gary Chapman, *best-selling author of* The Five Love Languages *and other books on marriage and family relationships, has served on the staff of Calvary Baptist Church in Winston-Salem, N.C., since 1971. He is a popular conference speaker. He and his wife, Karolyn, have been on several short-term missions trips, often to provide marriage enrichment training to missionaries throughout the world. The Chapmans have a son who is a missionary, a daughter who is a physician, and two grandchildren. Gary attended MBI's Undergraduate School 1955–58.*

4

HEAR THE CRIES
OF THEIR HEARTS

◆　　　◆　　　◆

T H E   S T O R Y   O F
R O N   H U T C H C R A F T

"It sounded like Niagara Falls." That's how the doctor described the sound as he listened with his stethoscope to the area around my wife's liver. At the time, Karen was battling an almost-fatal case of hepatitis, and the doctor said he could literally hear the roar of the blood racing to her liver to save it. It's a reflex of the human body to rush its life-saving resources to whatever part has the most desperate need.

Over the past several years, God has broken my heart for one of the greatest spiritual needs I have ever seen. In this case, I learned that the body of Christ is needed like never before to rush its life-saving resources to meet this need.

Here's my story.

When I was growing up on the South Side of Chicago, my family was "the lost." My parents gambled, smoked, and drank. We never went to church. We didn't know Jesus and didn't care.

But, when I was four years old, my family was reached by a missionary who never spoke a word. That silent missionary was my baby brother who died soon after birth. God used the death of my baby brother to soften my dad's heart, get his attention, and get him into a church. There we heard the Gospel and came to Christ.

God turned a seemingly senseless tragedy into an open door for life.

Four decades later, I stumbled upon another tragedy, and the more I looked into it, the more alarmed I became. In 1990, I was asked to speak for a Native American ministry in Window Rock, Arizona. I agreed, and we found a spot on the calendar several months out and set a date.

Forty-five minutes before I was scheduled to leave for this trip, I began to find out what I was getting into. A fax arrived. I glanced at the sheets of paper as they rolled out of the fax machine. *Who sent this?* There was no name. I started reading the statistics. "Suicide—four times the national average. . . . Grief—most nine-year-olds have buried three to five of their closest friends and family. . . ." I caught the phrase "the most devastated adolescents in America."

I thought to myself, *I've been in youth ministry twenty-five years. I've traveled all over the USA and in different parts of the world. I've worked in the inner cities of Chicago and New York City. I certainly know what some of the most devastated adolescents in America suffered through, but these young people are different. They are facing struggles that are unique.*

The report went on. These were not kids from Chicago or New York or any other inner city. These were kids on the reservation. Native American young people—the very people I was on my way to visit. I was stunned. I had no idea. But I had a plane to catch. I stuffed the fax into my briefcase and headed out the door.

I strolled through the airport, past the newsstand. I stopped, backed up, scanned the headlines, and handed over some coins. *Here it is again!* "Two-thirds of Native America is under age twenty-seven." With all that youth, I would expect to find a culture brimming with energy and life. Instead I read of sexual abuse, rape, alcoholism, drug abuse, despair, hopelessness, and suicide.

More airports, more newspapers, more headlines. Suddenly, everybody was talking about the crisis of Native American youth. However, this was more than just statistics to me—these were people who needed Jesus. *How could I have focused my whole life on youth ministry and missed these young people?* I thought I knew America's young people. But this group had completely eluded me. I knew more about youth in China and Russia than I did about the condition of our first Americans.

But what had been invisible was now coming into focus as a burning, blinding reality.

As my plane approached the Phoenix airport, we flew over some of these reservations, and I was moved to tears. From thousands of feet above, I observed the obvious desolation of these villages. My heart was broken for these American Indian young people.

This is catastrophic, I told myself, as the plane touched down. *What is the church doing about this?* When I got to Arizona, I called together missionaries and other friends who knew me from my radio program. I wanted their "take" on this report about Native American kids. I asked, "Seventy-eight percent of the population here are under the age of twenty-seven—what percentage of the ministry here is directed toward their young people?" It was pretty silent in the room. There was almost no such thing as youth ministry among "the most devastated adolescents in America."

Something was horribly wrong with this picture. *If these*

were the most desperate kids in America, you'd think we'd have the most dynamic youth ministry in America there. But that was not the case. Outside the reservation, it seemed that very few knew or cared. Somehow, American Indian young people had almost dropped off the radar screen of the church. They had fallen through the cracks and were completely forgotten. Inside the reservation, the church was perceived as irrelevant to most youth. The typical reservation church struggled with attendance of fewer than twenty people, most over fifty years old.

I discovered that young people on the reservation were largely an unreached people group. Not only were they unreached, but many considered them unreachable. The term "young Native American Christian" was almost an oxymoron.

On the flight home, I realized something unexpected, but defining, had happened to me. As I began journaling what I read and what I experienced on that reservation, I realized that these last few days would help define my ministry future.

I reasoned, *I have a full plate. I don't need anything else to do. We're already maxed out with radio ministry and evangelism outreaches. I have enough to keep me busy for the rest of my life.*

But God didn't let me off the hook.

My definition of a "call" is simple. A "call" is this: *I can't not do it!* It may be poor grammar, but it works. *I can't not do it.*

And I couldn't walk away from the call to minister to Native American youth. God had used this experience to break my heart for these young people. They are hungry for the Savior. They need the hope that Jesus has to offer.

My wife, Karen, and I prayed about the next logical step of making this an extension of our ongoing ministry. We had to find a way to do this. I've often said, "Knowledge equals responsibility," and this was an occasion for us to be obedient and respond to the need.

Now the problem was *how to reach them.* Like *my* family before Christ, these young people didn't know Jesus and they didn't care.

We knew this would be no easy task. The spiritual strongholds of the Native American world have been largely unchallenged for five hundred years. It is a stronghold of darkness with dysfunction as the norm. To set up a ministry to Native American youth would require a groundbreaking strategy. We knew it would cost; it would be expensive—emotionally, mentally, spiritually, and financially. Satan makes sure it costs.

It took the death of my little brother to reach my family. *What will it take to reach these youth?*

I had to look into the past to find the answer, because it was in the past that God wired me to cross cultures with the Gospel. I grew up with African-American kids in my neighborhood and school. We were in a changing area of Chicago. I realize now it was a tense neighborhood, but somebody forgot to tell the kids. The adults didn't tell us we weren't supposed to like each other. From an early age, I learned to build bridges with people from all kinds of backgrounds.

After graduating from Moody Bible Institute, I ministered in gang neighborhoods on the South Side of Chicago during the turbulent 1960s. Unrest over civil rights, the assassination of Dr. King, and growing American involvement in Vietnam bred conflict and violence.

On the streets of inner-city Chicago, I began to understand

that I must approach the young people I worked with in much the same way a missionary would. These young people were part of their own culture, their own "tribe," you could say. To reach them, I needed to ask the right questions. *What language do they speak? What does their culture care about? Where do I find members of that tribe?* I couldn't expect them to come to my "village." I needed to go to their village. I had to bring Christ to them, or they would not get this life-or-death message.

This strategy worked and it worked well—until 1970. That was the year God moved us to northern New Jersey to the suburbs of New York City. I tried duplicating what I had done on the South Side of Chicago, but it didn't work. It needed major adjustment for the New York City setting.

Wait a minute! What is wrong? I was the same guy, with the same gifts and the same strategy. But these young people spoke a different language. They didn't understand terms like "accept Christ," "personal Savior," "sin," "believe," "born again," or "saved." My "Christian vocabulary" was meaningless. At that time the Northeast was in the early stages of post-Christianity (which has since enveloped the entire nation). These young people had no reason to be interested in the Gospel. I couldn't assume they had any sense of having sinned, because they had no sense of boundaries. You can't be out-of-bounds if you don't think there are any boundaries. Sin was a nonissue to them. I had the same Great Commission, but a new culture, and I needed a new approach.

I got my plan by listening, which I realized was the key to crossing cultures. I quickly found out that I couldn't get Jesus through a closed door. Instead, I had to find the open door by listening to the cries of their hearts.

Once I found where their *need* was, where they were hurting, I could help these young people attach that need to the absence of God in their lives. Then they could begin to think about their relationship with Him.

As I continued to cross cultures, the cries changed, the open doors changed, and the methods changed with them. But some things stayed the same. The Gospel, of course, never changes. I also discovered another principle that seems to work in every culture: Young people listen to other young people.

This was the key. Karen and I were convinced of it. Young Native Americans would listen to other young Native Americans. The solution was on the reservation, but very few were using it.

In 1990, it was very hard to find young Native American Christians. It took quite a search to find some. But we did find a few, and we put them to work. We took our family vacation the next summer and devoted it to developing a strategy for reaching Native American youth with the Gospel. We put together a little team, trained them to present Christ, and went to some isolated spots on the Navajo reservation. The results were amazing.

I've seen creative, well-organized youth rallies and outreaches. By comparison, this was simple and spontaneous. Our Gospel presenters were not professional ministers, pastors, or evangelists. Instead, these were broken young people, simply telling about the hope that they have found in a relationship with the Creator God, through His Son, Jesus Christ. These Indian kids were quiet, passive, and far from outgoing. But they lived in the world of the most devastated adolescents in America. They shared their story with their peers, and more than one hundred of them came to Christ.

A veteran missionary stood next to me and said, "I never thought I'd live to see the day when Indian kids would bring Indian kids to Christ."

It hardly seemed to occur to anybody that the Native youth could do this.

But they did, and the strategy grew. What happened on that Navajo reservation has been repeated again and again on reservations throughout the Southwest. The ministry has grown into what is now called "On Eagles' Wings." Every summer, Native American young people travel to some of the spiritually darkest Native communities in North America. Often in a short time, three to four weeks, they have the privilege of leading six to seven hundred young Native Americans to Christ. Churches and missionaries are scrambling to keep up with the harvest. They've never seen anything like it before.

Broken Indian young people make it happen. Why do they have credibility with their peers? Because they've been the sexual abuse victims, the rape victims, the alcoholics, the drug abusers, and the gang members. They are the ones who've buried many of their loved ones before they were teenagers. Many have even attempted to take their own lives. When these young believers stand on the reservation basketball court and tell their stories, the other kids there can relate.

"Let me tell you where hope came from," they say. "Hope came from the Creator's Son. His name is Jesus Christ, a dark-skinned man from a tribe. His tribe was called Judah. He came from a people with ceremonies, living in a land that others had taken over. Sound familiar? This is not just a white man's Jesus like you thought He was. He's not just an old man's Jesus—He died for each one of us, and you can have a relationship with Jesus Christ beginning tonight."

When I listened to the cries of their hearts, for some reason, God shared part of His broken heart for the world with me. I am humbled and honored that God would use me to play a part in reaching Native Americans for Christ. As I look ahead, I realize there is so much more to be done, and I look forward to the challenges. Through much prayer, we anticipate that the best victories are yet to come!

♦   ♦   ♦

Ron Hutchcraft is an author and a speaker, radio host, and contemporary evangelist. As president of Ron Hutchcraft Ministries, Inc., Ron and his team facilitate citywide evangelistic outreaches, produce two radio programs ("A Word with You" for adults and "RealTime" to impact lost youth), the Website hutchcraft.com, and the "On Eagles' Wings" Native American outreach.

Ron was honored as Moody Bible Institute's Alumnus of the Year in 1997 (Undergraduate School 1962–65). Ron's ministry partner is his wife Karen, one of the greatest treasures he gained while a student at Moody. The Hutchcrafts have three grown children (all in full-time Christian ministry) and three grandchildren.

5

LESSONS FROM
THE INTERVIEW

◆   ◆   ◆

THE STORY OF
JERRY B. JENKINS

I stared at the blank screen.

No way I'm qualified to pull this off.

But Dr. Tim LaHaye and Tyndale House were counting
on me to write a novel about the end times. *How can I do
justice to the greatest cosmic event that will ever happen?* I had
already put off the project for a year to assist Billy Graham
with his memoirs.

I had written more than a hundred books and thousands
of articles. I laughed when people asked about writer's block.
"A factory worker can't call in and say, 'I'm having worker's
block.' Like him, I have a job. I sit down and do it."

But I had never been more aware of the poverty of my
own resources. This would be no normal book.

Dr. LaHaye wanted a novel directed to two audiences:
Christians and non-Christians. But that's not how it works, I
tried to tell him. I need one reader in mind. "A double-
minded book is unstable in all its ways," I said. But, no, he
wanted to reach both kinds of readers.

This is so much bigger than I am. How could I tell a story

many others had told, without sounding hokey? How could
I bring it to life so readers would finally understand Bible
prophecy?

◆   ◆   ◆

This wasn't the first time I had faced a challenge bigger
than I. Just over a year earlier, the president of the Billy Graham
Evangelistic Association contacted me about assisting Dr.
Graham with his memoirs. "What qualifies you to do this?"
was his final question.

"Nothing," I said. "Who would be qualified? All a writer
can do is the best he can do."

I spent the next twelve months traveling back and forth to
North Carolina to interview Dr. Graham and help put together
much of what went into his autobiography, *Just As I Am.*

How did Dr. Graham handle challenges like I was facing? Such obstacles were a daily experience for him, yet
somehow he handled them. And, unlike many celebrities, he
was the same man behind closed doors that he was on the
platform. Was he cut from different stock than the rest of us,
or did he possess some secret we could learn?

I posed that question to him one day in his modest office
in Montreat, North Carolina. It was 1993, and at seventy-
four he was thin and frail.

I began, "The people in the evangelical community look
at you as their spiritual leader . . ."

He waved me off. "They shouldn't do that."

"Well, they do," I said. "In fact, you've been described as
the Protestant Pope . . ."

He shook his head. "People shouldn't put me on a
pedestal."

"But they do," I said, "and people see you as an example of how to live."

He leaned out of his chair and pressed his hand flat on the floor. "When I think of how many times I've failed the Lord," he said, "I feel this low."

Billy Graham?

But his answer wasn't out of character. His response to a standing ovation from a stadium full of people? Dr. Graham looked down. He didn't wave. He just sat. Dr. Graham's response was so different from that of many star athletes and celebrities. Most light up when they come into contact with people. They come into a room expecting the spotlight.

I asked, "Doesn't it warm your heart when a crowd thanks you like that?"

"No, I just hate it. The Bible says God will share His glory with no other, and I don't want any of that."

"But can't you see that the people are not glorifying you but rather God by thanking you?"

Dr. Graham said, "I would just rather dig a hole and climb into it."

Now I sat in his office wondering how to get at something the average reader could take away. I tried, "How do you maintain your own spiritual disciplines?"

Finally he grew animated. "It's no secret. The Bible doesn't make it hard. We are told to do two things: to pray without ceasing and search the Scriptures daily."

I had always hoped the "pray without ceasing" line from Paul was figurative, because I certainly hadn't been able to pull it off.

I said, "You pray without ceasing?"

Dr. Graham looked me in the eye and said, "I do. And I have every waking moment since I received Christ as a teenager. I'm praying right now that everything I say is honoring to God and not to me."

So much for something readers can identify with.

"How about searching the Scriptures?" I said. "What form does that take?"

He said, "Wherever I am in the world, I put my Bible where I can see it during the course of the day. If I'm in a hotel room, I open it and put it on the bed. If I'm in my office, I open it and put it on the edge of my desk. If I'm at home I put it someplace where I'm going to see it frequently."

I looked over his shoulder. There it was, his open Bible on the desk.

"Anytime I notice that open Bible, I stop and read a verse or two, a chapter or two, or I read for an hour or two. This is not for sermon preparation. It's just for my own edification. It's my spiritual food."

Now we're getting somewhere. Everybody wants to have a daily devotional time and make it work. "How do you get back into it if you miss a day or two?"

He cocked his head and squinted. "I don't think I've ever done that."

"You've never missed a day?!"

"No," he said. "I told you. It's my spiritual food."

That night I was still thinking about what he had said. People often ask, "What's the difference with Billy Graham? There are better preachers and better theologians, but his ministry has been so blessed over the years. Whenever he preaches, thousands come to Christ."

As he said, it was no secret. Pray without ceasing. Search the Scriptures. Two simple things anyone can do. The difference is: He does it.

And it shows in his prayers. When he prayed over Mexican food, I felt I was eating the most blessed tacos I'd ever had.

His wife, Ruth, said that when she first heard him pray at Wheaton College sixty years ago, she told a friend, "I don't know who that is, but he sure sounds like he knows Who he's talking to."

◆   ◆   ◆

As I sat before that empty computer screen, wondering how to begin what would become the Left Behind series, I could only pray.

In that moment of overwhelming inadequacy, the Scripture I learned growing up in a Bible church, the Scripture reinforced while I was a student at Moody Bible Institute, reminded me that this project didn't depend upon me. James 4:10 says, "Humble yourselves in the sight of the Lord, and He will lift you up."

It didn't take much to humble myself that day. At the end of myself, I needed God to remind me that He had prepared me for this, that it was a rare privilege. I knew from Psalm 55:22 that I could cast my cares upon the Lord and He would sustain me. If I trusted the Lord, I need not dwell on my inadequacies.

◆   ◆   ◆

I've written more than 150 books, but things are different whenever I write one of the Left Behind novels. My wife, Dianna, says she can always tell when a deadline for Left Behind is coming because I'll get sick, I'll get tired, I'll have an injury, my computer will go on the fritz, whatever.

Why? I believe it's because so many thousands have told us that they have received Christ through reading these stories. That can't be something the Enemy likes. I feel the oppression. I may get enough sleep, eat right, work out. Yet when I sit down to work on Left Behind, I feel like I could sleep for a year. Fighting through the work is like war.

I'm back to square one, again at the end of my own resources. Whatever gifts I have are inadequate to the task. There is no way I can do it alone. If God doesn't show up, the work is beyond me.

◆　　　◆　　　◆

The Left Behind series has succeeded beyond any expectations. But when I think of success, I think of something I learned as a young man before Dianna and I had children. I was working at Scripture Press. I interviewed four or five middle-aged men (about twice my age), each on a different topic, each for a different story.

One question, however, came up in every interview. "Do you have any regrets?" I asked.

To a man, they all said the same thing. "I wish I had spent more time with my kids when they were growing up."

These were good men, their children good people. None of their kids had left the faith or gone off the deep end. But the men shared the same sorrow; something precious had been lost and could never be recovered.

I told Dianna, "I think God is trying to tell me something. If I get to that age and have the same regret, I'll be without excuse."

So even before we had our first child, Dianna and I set a policy: From the time I came home from work until the time the kids went to bed, I would do no writing or office work. I would be there for my children. Dianna also made that time a priority. I did all my writing between nine o'clock and midnight, after the kids went to bed. And we maintained that policy for all three boys.

When our neighbor came home from work, his kids ran to him, hugged him, celebrated him. I felt jealous. My kids were taking me for granted.

Then it hit me. He was celebrated because his kids never knew when he was going to be home or for how long. My kids considered it normal for me to be there every day to play with them. In reality, they were paying me the highest compliment.

The benefits of our policy were all mine. I was there when all three of my boys received Christ. I heard firsthand the funny things that kids say at different ages.

When my youngest son's fifth-grade basketball team lost a game, he told me, "It wasn't fair. The other team had a player with hair under his arms."

I said, "That *doesn't* sound fair. How old was he?"

"They said he was only twelve," Mike said, "but he's already been through poverty."

I wouldn't trade moments like that.

The result has been great friendships with our boys. Like all kids, they sometimes disagreed with us or argued with us, but they never once questioned our motives, because maintaining that policy proved to them how much they meant to us.

Eldest son Dallas puts it like this: "You didn't just tell us we were your top priority. You proved it every day."

To me, that is success.

◆   ◆   ◆

*Jerry B. Jenkins, author of the Left Behind series, has written
more than 150 books. He owns Jenkins Entertainment, a film-
making company, and the Christian Writers Guild. Jerry is the
former vice president of publishing at Moody and is Moody's
"Writer-At-Large." He also serves on the Institute's board of
trustees. He attended the Undergraduate School 1967–68. He
and his wife, Dianna, live in Colorado. They have three grown
sons and one grandson. Regarding the success of the Left Behind
series, he says: "I tell the guys I'm accountable to, 'If I ever, ever
act like I deserve any of this, just punch me in the mouth.'" Visit
www.jerryjenkins.com to learn more about him and his work.*

6

I AM
NOT ASHAMED

• • •

"If you want to reach the world, stay here in Chicago."
No way, I thought. *I'm going back to Spain.*
"The world has come to our doorstep. The nations have come to our American cities."
My pastor's suggestions shocked me. *Stay in Chicago? I don't like Chicago.*

I grew up on the mission field in a village of two hundred people in northern Spain. From fourth to eighth grade, I walked dirt roads to attend a one-room schoolhouse. For me, the idea of urban ministry meant visiting nearby Burgos, Spain, to chat with university students. Coming to Chicago at age seventeen to attend Moody Bible Institute was all the culture shock I wanted.

As soon as I can, I'm going back to Spain.

Those were my intentions, but I couldn't get out of my head this little voice that said, *Maybe God doesn't always call us where we're comfortable.* Even after I graduated from Moody and went on to a different college, God pulled me back to Chicago.

My girlfriend was there. And I needed to keep my Spanish sharp. So I took a summer job at National Can in Chicago, and I connected with a little church in an inner-city neighborhood on the Southwest side.

I was taken aback by what I saw that summer. I saw my first stabbing. I saw a shoot-out. I witnessed a gang fight right in front of the place where I was staying. I saw a fifteen-year-old pregnant girl get stabbed by a rival gang member.

As I worked on the assembly line, putting tops and bottoms on cans, I processed these experiences in prayer. "I hate the city," I told God.

But the more I complained, the more I felt Him challenging my heart. *Will you just endure the city?* God seemed to be asking. *Or will you embrace it and love the people I love in it?*

I wrestled with that for a long time. Finally I said, "OK, God. I'll love whatever You want me to love. If You want me to love the city, I'll love the city."

From that point forward, God changed my attitude. Instead of seeing a city I hated, I saw people and families that God loved.

I knew I needed to do something; I needed to take some kind of action. So I went to the people in charge of the little mission church I was attending and said, "I want to help out. I'm willing, when I graduate from school, to come here and help out for a year. I will help you do whatever you need done."

They smiled. Their little church of eighteen people had been without a pastor for almost three years.

"Be our pastor," they said.

Oh, no! I thought. *I'm not interested in the pastorate. You have the wrong guy. I majored in communications at Moody, not pastoral studies. I'm on my way to Spain to use drama to creatively evangelize. I can't be your pastor.*

But, deep down inside, I knew God wanted me to say yes. So I said, "Yes. I'll be your pastor."

I returned in December 1985. My church consisted of women, children, and four men: two gypsies, a sixty-seven-year-old recovering alcoholic, and a young Hispanic fresh out of the Marines. The first person I led to Christ was a Puerto Rican former drug dealer who couldn't come to church because he was doing community service.

They started me on a salary of $8,000 a year, which was all they could afford. One of the members owned an old office building, so he let me have a room there. I slept on a mattress on the floor with a ring of mousetraps around it. I looked out my window at night and saw gangs fighting. I had no health insurance. I drove an old beat-up car. I could barely pay the bills.

What am I doing here? I asked myself. *God, is this really where I'm supposed to be?*

In this context, as a twenty-one-year-old novice pastor, tucked away in a forgotten part of the city, I received a very interesting phone call.

"Rev. Jobe," the caller said. "We need a minister to offer the invocation and benediction at our college graduation ceremony. This event will be held at the prestigious Rockefeller Memorial Chapel on the University of Chicago campus."

Wow! They're asking me?!

I agreed.

When I arrived, I could see that this was a very proper, sophisticated, almost liturgical type of ceremony. The setting was beautiful and ornate. Everything about it exuded power, wealth, and influence. The chapel itself was designed and built at the request of the university's founder, John D. Rockefeller, to be the "central and dominant feature" of the campus. And, of course, nobody needed to tell me that the University of Chicago is one of the world's premier universities, home of the intellectual elite.

By contrast, I was ministering in a squalor of a tiny, barely emerging, almost storefront little ghetto church.

Why did they ask me?

Wearing cap and gown, I joined the president of the college and the other deans, and we began to march toward the front where we would face graduates and visitors from all over the world.

As we were marching, the master of ceremonies turned to me and said, "Rev. Jobe, we are so glad you are here to pray at this graduation ceremony. You realize that businessmen from all over the world and family members have come to this graduation. It's very important. Of course, you realize that this is a nonsectarian event. People from many different faiths are here today. We would very much appreciate it if you would try to keep your prayers as nonsectarian as possible."

I almost stopped marching. "What exactly does that mean?" I asked him.

He smiled. "You are an educated man. We know that you are a smart young man. You understand the need to refrain from any language that would make this sectarian— words like 'Jesus Christ' and so forth. You can have your faith; we just don't want anybody to feel uncomfortable."

There was no way to leave. We were marching up the aisle. I said, "I really wish someone would have told me that before I was asked to pray."

"We understand that," he said. "We have heard that you are a very intelligent young man and that you would understand the setting."

Without further ado, they ushered me onstage.

There we were—all onstage—each in his appropriate place. The master of ceremonies made a few opening remarks about the distinguished invited guests, individuals with Ph.D.'s, with impressive accomplishments. Meanwhile, I looked over the crowd. Everyone was in suit and tie. Clearly, the visitors represented every major people group from India to secular America.

Then the master of ceremonies said, "This is Rev. Jobe. He's going to provide the invocation."

I walked slowly to the podium and looked at the assembled audience. All kinds of thoughts raced through my mind. *Sure. I am an intelligent guy. I do understand the setting. I'm not in an insignificant little place in Southwest Chicago anymore. I'm on the University of Chicago campus. This is my opportunity to speak before some very influential people.*

I did what they asked me to do. I prayed a very generic prayer. I used the word "God" but not "Lord." I never mentioned the name "Jesus." I made my prayer nonsectarian, just like they wanted.

Then I sat down.

The moment I sat down, I began to realize what I had done. Anyone who has ever been under the convicting power of the Holy Spirit will understand what I felt. I don't know what the temperature was in the Rockefeller Chapel that day, but I was burning up. My face was turning red. The Holy Spirit was reminding me of a verse I had memorized long before: "I am not ashamed of the gospel of Christ, for it is the power of God to salvation" (Romans 1:16).

I felt the Spirit of God saying to me, *If you don't pray in Jesus' name, what kind of prayer are you praying?*

What have I done? I had allowed the pressure of a secular

environment and my own desire for significance to compromise the ministry God gave me.

The struggle inside was so intense that I was oblivious to whatever else was happening in that ceremony—Dr. So-and-So, Prestigious So-and-So, this invited guest, that distinguished author—they went on and on.

Finally, the master of ceremonies stood up and said, "Now for our benediction, we invite again, Rev. Jobe."

By that time, I was ready. I double-stepped it to that podium. When I got up to pray, I knew exactly what I was going to say. With trembling in my voice but holy courage swelling up inside of me, I said, "I understand that this is a nonsectarian event. And my goal is not to offend anybody. But I will close with the benediction and pray in the only name I know how to pray in, and that is the name of Jesus Christ."

I knew that the college president and the dean were shrinking beside me; I didn't want to look back and see their faces. But I prayed, and I prayed with fervor. I used the name of Jesus three or four times just to make sure I was making up for the first prayer. I prayed with fire. I prayed with passion. I prayed with conviction. I asked God to bless those students. I asked that they would sense and come to know Him. Then I closed my prayer, "In the name of Jesus. Amen."

Silence. The entire auditorium was still.

I walked back to my seat. I could feel the tension onstage. The master of ceremonies returned to the podium. He stuttered and said, "OK, we are dismissed."

I didn't wait to say "hello" to the president. I didn't wait to congratulate anybody. I just started down that aisle, walking as quickly as I could, making my way toward the back.

But I didn't make it to the back. A girl jumped out in front of me, waving. "Pastor Jobe! Pastor Jobe!"

Oh no! Here it comes, I thought.

She stopped me in the middle of the aisle and said, "I'm a student here. I'm graduating today. I want to thank you for praying according to your convictions, for using the name of Jesus. I've never heard it used in any of our ceremonies. Thank you. It was refreshing to hear someone pray without being ashamed."

With those words of encouragement, I walked away.

That was a turning point in my life. As I wrestled between the desire to be significant and the desire to be obedient, God helped me to understand that the greatest success was saying yes to God. I began to realize that the Gospel is simple but powerful. Secular culture will try to squeeze our convictions and try to squeeze the message right out of our ministry so it becomes generic, nonoffensive, and ineffective.

I went home and prayed, "God, I will never, ever be ashamed or compromise the message of the Gospel of Jesus Christ simply to try to fit in. I will follow the call of Christ, whether anybody else knows my name or not. Even if I spend the rest of my life at a little storefront church, ministering to the outcasts of society, even if I never return to Spain, I believe the greatest success in life is simply saying yes to You."

I could have easily begun to compromise to remain socially acceptable. But God showed me how important it was to remain true to the call of God in my life. As a result of this lesson, the leaders in our church have been up front in all of our ministry about the message of Christ. We have called people to a strong commitment, an up-front discipleship. We have seen hundreds and hundreds of people come to

Jesus Christ as Lord and Savior—not just the marginal people of society, but businesspeople, university students, and professionals. All classes of people have been touched by the Gospel of Jesus Christ.

◆   ◆   ◆

God had another lesson for me during that first year of ministry. Since our church was so small, I felt like everything rested on me. If anything was going to be done, I would make it happen. That seemed to work OK until I got sick.

I was sick for an entire week. All week I could barely swallow. I had lumps in the back of my throat. On Sunday I got up. *I have to preach.* I prayed, *O God, don't let me faint or pass out in the pulpit.* I was sweating. I was hot. I could barely stand.

After the service, I was persuaded to go to get medical attention. Since I had no health insurance, my grandmother's doctor agreed to see me.

"You have strep throat. You have mono. And it looks like you have a touch of hepatitis. You are completely worn out," he said.

I spent the next week flat on my back in bed.

God was speaking to my heart. *You are not the messiah. I want you doing less and praying more. What I'm about to do is not about you; it is about My power working through broken vessels.*

I began to see that God was far more interested in brokenness than He was in my tenacity, my personality, my power, or my persuasion. I started to understand that this ministry was "not by might nor by power, but by [God's] Spirit" (Zechariah 4:6 NIV). I determined to pray more, to let God do what I cannot do. I decided to follow the way of brokenness. I concluded it was better to follow the rules of the spiritual world than to try to operate by the rules of the natural world. I wrote in my prayer journal, "Those who go ahead of God are full of pride and self. Those who lag behind God are full of fear and doubt. Let me go right in step with You."

This became a pattern for our ministry. As a church we acknowledge our own dependence and weakness before God. We set aside times to fast and pray, coming to God and saying, "God, we understand that we don't have the power, the money, the strength, or the talent to accomplish the vision You've called us to. We are operating from a place of weakness. We are calling out to You."

The result has been miraculous. Our little church of eighteen has grown to seventeen hundred, meeting in eight locations in nine services every Sunday. Most of our growth has been new conversions to Christ. We are a multi-racial, multi-lingual, multi-ethnic fellowship called New Life Community Church.

God has given us a vision to reach 1 percent of Chicago, or thirty thousand people. When God gave us that vision, we began asking ourselves, *If we are going to reach thirty thousand people in the city of Chicago, what is that going to look like?* We realized at once that it won't be a stadium. We won't wait for the people to come to us; we will go to them. We realized this church must be in multiple locations. It must speak multiple languages. It must raise leaders. It must be vibrant in evangelism, powerful in prayer, and regularly fasting.

Three times a year we come together to one location for a combined worship celebration. The result is a multicultural experience in which a twenty-nine-year-old computer geek who lives in a plush part of the city worships side by side with an immigrant who can barely speak English and who washes dishes at a restaurant where the computer consultant meets his contacts for lunch.

Now churches are contacting us, offering to donate their buildings, asking to merge their congregations into New Life. These groups were thriving in the 1940s, but now they struggle to survive in the face of urban change. God has given us a strategy to rebirth these congregations into a vibrant new church, relevant to the neighborhood, true to the Gospel.

And although long ago I gave God my dream of returning to Spain, He has given it back to me. My ministry has released me enough so I can go back and forth to Spain, pretty much when I want to, and be involved there. We have sent out a fully supported team of missionaries to Spain. And I personally get the opportunity to minister there three or four times a year. Our youth conference ministry has grown to be the largest in Spain. I've had the opportunity to work with drama and other creative means of communicating the Gospel in that nation.

I gave my dream to God, and He gave it back to me. God does that. He satisfies our desires with good things (Psalm 103:5).

◆   ◆   ◆

Mark Jobe is the senior pastor of the rapidly growing New Life Community Church. He is also adjunct professor of Urban Issues at Moody Bible Institute. He and his wife, Dee, have three young children. Mark attended Moody's Undergraduate School 1981–84, and he got his master's degree at the Graduate School in 1998.

7

LIFE *IS*
MINISTRY

◆　　◆　　◆

We had no food. Breakfast was over and there was no more food. We had no idea how our campers would get fed that day. Nothing for lunch. Nothing for supper. No money to buy anything.

In the camping business, this is not a good thing. Meals are part of the package.

It defied words. I couldn't believe it.

I looked at the camp director, Marshall Williams. He and his wife knew we were out of food, but they didn't seem worried. Not a bit.

Like everyone else on staff, I sat at the table, bowed my head, and joined the directors in prayer. Simple prayers. No bells and whistles. We just quietly asked our heavenly Father to supply what we needed for that day.

In spite of the need, there was an unusual calm in that room. Instead of panic, there was a sense of expectancy. "We are partners with God," the director said. "He is in this ministry with us. It isn't our job to worry about how we are going to get food. God knows. And He will take care of it."

This was new to me. Though I grew up with seven broth-ers and sisters, though I knew what it meant for things to be tight, I had never experienced anything like this before.

We finished praying and went about our activities. Later that morning, the mailman arrived right on schedule. One of the campers ran down to the mailbox. He returned from the mailbox yelling, "It looks like somebody sent a check!" The staff gathered, read the letter, and looked at the check. "God answered our prayers just in time," Marshall com-mented as he got into his car to drive into town to deposit the check in the bank. On his way back, he picked up gro-ceries so the kids would have food for the day.

I had always heard about faith ministry, but I never expe-rienced it until I met this family. I lived with them and saw firsthand what it meant. It was simple. In fact, it seemed *too* simple. Ministry was who they were and how they lived. Their faith was the real deal, and it rubbed off on their chil-dren and on us staff members.

I spent twelve weeks at the Bible Witness Camp, learn-ing what was essential and what was not. I had a bed, three meals a day, and got to shop at the missionary barrel for my clothes. I learned that I didn't need much more than that. I grew content with the idea of the basics—shelter, food, and clothes. I left that camp with the life-changing realization that *my life was all about ministry* and that I didn't have to worry how I would be able to make it. God would sustain me no matter how bleak things got.

I decided to live by faith.

Living by faith was not on the top ten list of qualities most women sought out in relationships. Yet the Lord gave me a wonderful wife and a partner in ministry. Beth and I met as students at Moody Bible Institute. We came from similar family backgrounds and had the same heart for ministry. We worked together first in the Big Brother/Big Sister program, then later in Youth for Christ (YFC). We married soon after graduation, and I continued my work with YFC. From the very beginning, I never took my marriage with Beth for granted. We minister as a team. She is a genuine partner.

◆   ◆   ◆

YFC grew into a vibrant urban ministry in the Chicago high schools on the South and West Sides. Like all staff, I agreed to raise my own support, which I found to be a real challenge. I found out the hard way that I could not do that and missed many, many paychecks. Besides the finances, problems with the home office were troubling us toward the end of our seventeen years with YFC.

However, God was quick to solve both problems. He led us to step out on faith to form a brand-new ministry called the Chicago Urban Reconciliation Enterprise (CURE). Oh, you'd better believe we had our doubts about doing this, wondering how we were going to survive and get paid. But we knew that God wanted us to do something different. And we've seen through the years since we made that decision that He has proven faithful. The ministry is growing, and our financial situation has almost completely turned around. We rarely miss a paycheck. But it took our stepping out to a new level of faith for us to find His will. We trust God to meet our needs, and He does so in unique ways.

Those tight early years in ministry did test my faith in God's ability to provide. Folks say to me even today, "How do you guys do it? I can't figure it out. I literally can't figure out how you guys are surviving."

And yet we have plenty. We're quick to say that God has really done it. Through the years, He's kept us trusting Him. I always come back to my experience at Bible Witness Camp. If God could sustain the Williamses and their ministry, He can sustain me. No, God has not always given us a regular salary. But He doesn't need to. He's far too creative to be confined to one way of providing. Instead, He finds many ways to fill our lives with unexpected blessings.

God does the providing. But we have a role as well. Thrift, humility, and generosity are our responsibility. From our upbringing, Beth and I both learned how to stretch the dollar and make money go further. We knew how to shop when things were tight. God has been so generous to us, and we seek to share His generosity with our neighbors. Why should I have all kinds of material possessions when the people I work with have so little? My friends say, "You're never going to have anything, because whenever you get something, you give it away." But that's how we operate. I'm afraid to live any other way. Living by faith and being generous to others has always worked. I'm not sure that any other way would work for us. My wife and I have not had a vacation for four years. We were planning a vacation this year, but needs came up in the family, and the money we had put aside for vacation met those needs. We believe if God shows a person a need, he should get involved.

We live by faith, and our ministry grows out of our lives. For example, since 1986 we've run an operation after school called the Homework Club. That idea emerged the first year we were in our new neighborhood. Kids wanted our children to come out and play after school. Beth told them, "Sure, but they have to do their homework first. You can come in and do your homework too." Eventually that practice developed into a neighborhood club where kids who are registered can come after school and do homework. We have the tools, such as computers, books, paper, and pencils—whatever they need. Beth works with sixteen different kids, Monday through Thursday. That's the core piece of the ministry out of the home.

Children from our neighborhood come to our house and think we're rich. They see two television sets, two computers, and a lot of books—all tools for the Homework Club. They think we're rich, but we say, "No, we're not. We got this stuff from friends who help us do what we do." People who support our ministry have donated most of it.

God grows this ministry. For example, we bought the double city lot next to us for one dollar. We converted it into a playground for the neighborhood. We have a climbing structure for small kids and a sand volleyball court for older ones. Through the Lord's provision, we were able to buy the materials and install all of it with the help of friends.

Our home is also a hospitality house. People who are traveling from all over the world come and stay with us in our home in the neighborhood of South Chicago. Sometimes they are in town taking a course at one of the colleges or seminaries or attending a special conference such as Promise Keepers. We love welcoming and hosting people. Our doorbell rings all day long—people are constantly coming by. We're the "go to" place. If somebody needs something, even a bandage, they come to our house. It would drive some people crazy, but this is how we live. Some people think this a spiritual gift. For us, it's just a way of life. It's who we are. It's no big deal. We feel God gave the house to us, and He wants us to use it as a ministry outreach tool. The same is true with our car or anything else we have. It's a tool for ministry.

Recently a Haitian family across the street celebrated the ninety-fifth birthday of the grandfather, and afterward they brought over all kinds of leftover food. It was delicious! Do you know why they did this? We've been there for them, giving all the time. When they needed to leave their house after a fire, we offered them ours. I was taking off that very day for a speaking engagement, so Beth and I decided to let them use our house. They ended up needing the house for one week. And when you hear them talk about it, it's funny. They exaggerate: "We lived with Russ and Beth for a month." It makes us chuckle, but we are pleased that we were able to help them out. God has allowed us to help families in need like this many times. It's just a matter of being a good neighbor. We want our neighbors to see God through us.

When we moved to this neighborhood, we asked God for a house in a location where we could use it as a ministry to our neighbors. God honored our request by giving us neighbors in crisis. We were placed here to represent who God is. As good neighbors, that's our task. People don't know God. That's why He places each of us where He has, so folks will know who He is by those of us who are His representatives. We model to a watching world how a good neighbor lives.

The kids in the Homework Club ask us, "Why do y'all do this? Why do you have this Homework Club at your house?" We say, "We are Christians, and God has been very generous and good to us, and He asked that we be generous with others." We don't need to pull out the flannelgraph board and give a formal presentation of the Gospel at regularly scheduled times. Instead, we find many opportunities to share our faith and talk about God in context of our relationship with these kids. We never need to do anything formal. We just try to be who we're supposed to be.

For many, ministry is a "profession." It is a compartment in their lives. They open it when it's convenient and close it when they want to. We don't take that approach. We focus on being authentic. This is who we are. Ministry is my life, and it is a walk of faith. I don't know how to do it any other way.

◆   ◆   ◆

Russ Knight *(Undergraduate School 1962–65, 1969–70) is president of Chicago Urban Reconciliation Enterprise (CURE). Russ and his partners provide consulting services to enhance reconciliation between individuals, organizations, and Christians of different races. Russ and his wife, Beth, have three children, a daughter-in-law, and a brand-new grandchild.*

8

MY GRACE IS
SUFFICIENT FOR YOU

◆   ◆   ◆

THE STORY OF
IAN LEITCH

"Hey, son, come here."

I looked over at Frank, wondering what was on his mind. I was working in the printing department of a big Scottish map publisher. It was Friday afternoon at quitting time, and I was anxious to get going. *What could he want?*

I walked over to where he was washing his hands. "Yes?" I said.

He continued, "Weren't you going to go into the ministry?"

"Well, yes," I said sheepishly. For ten years I had wanted nothing else. I dreamed of going to Bible college, of crossing the ocean, of attending Moody Bible Institute in Chicago, USA. When I was dating Morag, the woman who became my wife, I told her, "If we stay together, you had better be willing to go into the ministry at any time, in any place, at any cost." With all the enthusiasm of a fifteen-year-old, she answered, "I will." Now we were married, in our midtwenties, and nowhere closer to Bible college than we had been back then.

Bible school was the next step, but it seemed like an unattainable dream. I never went further than tenth grade in school. *They'll never let me in,* I thought. *Maybe Bible school won't be necessary,* I fantasized. *What if Billy Graham needs help right here in Scotland?* Billy Graham inspired me. I had heard him at an evangelistic crusade in Glasgow, Scotland, when I was sixteen. Later, I drew a map of Scotland and figured out where I would open Christian centers all over the nation. I was part of a band that went into coffee bars and cellar clubs to spread the Gospel. *I'm already doing the work of an evangelist . . . sort of.*

Frank looked me in the eye and brought me back to my senses. "Son, let me tell you something. If you don't move now, you'll never do it."

I couldn't believe my ears. Frank, a nice guy, yes, but certainly not a Christian—you could call him a pleasant pagan —was telling me to quit my job and get into the ministry!

I went home and talked to Morag. We started to pray seriously. *Maybe this is God's will. Maybe this printer is God's messenger. Maybe I should go to Bible college. But how will we ever do it? We are needed here.*

And we were needed. Morag's mother was not well. She was bedridden with rheumatoid arthritis. In Morag's memory, Mother had only gone outdoors with her twice, and both times Mother needed to be pushed in a wheelchair. *Who would care for Mother?*

My parents were getting up in years also. My brother suffered from emotional difficulties, and he had just experienced a bad spell in the hospital. *How can our parents cope without us?* With the Atlantic Ocean between us, we could not run home and help with every emergency.

Yet the call of God tugged at my heart. I had tasted the

work of an evangelist, and I loved it. Seeing missionary slides, hearing Billy Graham and other great speakers such as Oswald Smith, Herbert Lockyer, Tom Rees, and Hyman Appleman fueled my growing desire to serve in full-time ministry. If I stayed in secular employment, I would be forever restless and dissatisfied, knowing that God had a different plan for me.

When I was seventeen, I attended a concert that the Moody Chorale was performing in its first tour to the United Kingdom. After that event, I knew God wanted me to get my training at Moody and to return to Scotland as an evangelist. Now I was twenty-five. *Frank is right. Time is running out.*

We prayed and I struggled with the decision. *How do I reconcile this call with the realities of our family situation and my lack of education?*

A few Sundays later, I was still wondering what to do, when, driving away from church, my pastor, Dr. Alan Redpath, honked his horn and called us over. He looked me straight in the eye.

"I always find it easy to know God's will for other people. He wants you in the ministry." He rolled up the window and drove off.

I guess it can't hurt to apply to Moody Bible Institute. The worst they can do is say no. I applied.

How I got accepted was a complete mystery to me for years. Evidently it was a mystery to others too, because students and professors said to me, "You don't have an education. How did you get in?" I gave them the only answer I could think of.

"I just came through the Arch."[1]

I didn't find out until years later why Moody accepted

me as a student. When I graduated, one of the deans called me into his office. "Close the door," he said. "I'm not supposed to show this to you, but I thought you might want to read it. Here's what Alan Redpath said about you in his reference. Would you like to read it?"

I read it and smiled. His reference got me in the door.

But when I applied to Moody and was accepted, Morag and I were overjoyed and apprehensive. *How do we break the news to our parents?* I wondered. This was a struggle for us. *Will they think we've deserted them? Will they be angry? Will they support our decision?*

Working up the courage to speak to our parents was not easy. But God encouraged us with verses such as "[His] strength is made perfect in weakness" (2 Corinthians 12:9b), "casting all your care upon Him, for He cares for you" (1 Peter 5:7), and "no good thing will He withhold from those who walk uprightly" (Psalm 84:11b). We struggled with this decision, and, in the end, God's promise, "My grace is sufficient for you" (2 Corinthians 12:9a) helped us gain the peace we needed to discuss our decision with them.

Morag went to talk to her mother, and I went to talk to her dad in another part of the house.

Here unfolded a strange story I never expected. My father-in-law explained to me that he had been trained to go to China with the China Inland Mission. He was ready to go to China. But when he asked his girlfriend to marry him, she said, "Aren't you going to the mission field?"

"Yes," he said.

"Well, I'm not," she said. "I've never been called to the mission field."

He married his girlfriend, and she became my wife's mother.

My father-in-law said to me, "I said no to the mission field. You are taking over where I left off."

While I felt sad because he had said no to God's call, I also felt glad that the Lord had worked it out for good, so that I could meet and marry my life's partner. And I was so relieved by my father-in-law's kindness, warmth, and encouragement. We needed that encouragement more than they could imagine.

Meanwhile, Morag spoke with her mother. Morag's mother was joyous. She cried. "I'm so happy and so glad," she said over and over.

Their encouragement and release were a wonderful confirmation to us that we were in the Lord's will.

Now it was time to meet with my parents. My dad, the optimist of the family, beamed with excitement. He saw this as a wonderful opportunity. This was in character for him. When I was growing up, my dad worked at a fruit market. He took it upon himself to encourage everyone. He always had a "thought for the day." Many people, including several nuns, came back to him time after time to ask him for his "thought for the day." When people asked me if my father taught me the faith, I answered, "No, he lived it."

Mum was a different story. "You've failed everything," she said. "Whatever makes you think you'll pass now?"

"I don't know," I cried.

Then she told her biggest fear. "You'll never come back to Scotland," she said. "You'll stay in America and never come home."

Mum never did change her mind. She cried every time I stopped by the house before we left. In fact, she continued to naysay our time of training in Chicago until her death in 1981. It wasn't a matter of whether she was a Christian; she just didn't hold the same convictions and goals that we did. Perhaps, deep down, Mum knew we made the right decision but was never willing to admit it.

Upon selling our home, we stayed with Morag's parents for the last month before we moved to Chicago. Her mother said to her, "Now, Morag, on the day you leave, I don't want you to cry. I want to remember you smiling."

When that day came, they hugged, we prayed, and Morag smiled. Our last image of her mother remains fixed in my mind—waving with her crippled hand and smiling.

We walked outside. Morag wept.

◆   ◆   ◆

Those early months at Moody were difficult. The distance from Scotland was great, and communication options were limited. Telephone calls had to be booked in advance. E-mail was unheard of.

One bitterly cold January morning, six months after we arrived in Chicago, I received a message that a telegram was waiting for me at Crowell Hall desk. I was still in my bathrobe, watching Morag cross the street from our residence in Osborne Hall to the bus stop to await her bus to her job at the Quaker Oats Company. I shouted across the street, "Morag, would you go and pick up a telegram at Crowell Hall desk?"

We both intuitively knew the contents of that telegram before we opened it. Morag returned to our apartment with the telegram, and we opened it together.

"Mummy died last night," it said. Morag's mother's fight with rheumatoid arthritis was over. She was in heaven.

That same morning, before the telegram, in our devotions together we read the verse, "You will keep him in perfect peace, whose mind is stayed on You" (Isaiah 26:3).

As we were reading it, Morag said, "That's Mummy's favorite text."

When we got the news, Morag was crying, but through her tears she said, "Isn't God good? He gave me her favorite verse today."

We reread the telegram and noticed by its date that it had laid at Crowell Hall desk for three days, and somehow word never got to us that it was waiting. Initially, I was concerned about this poor service, but then the realization hit us: *The funeral is over.* Had we received it on time, we would have had three days to fret about not being able to travel four thousand miles to make it home for the funeral.

◆   ◆   ◆

As I neared graduation, Fairfield Avenue Baptist Church, a congregation I had been serving as a student pastor, asked me to become their full-time pastor. Suddenly, we needed to revisit the reason we came to Moody in the first place.

What a difficult decision! We loved America and still do. This opportunity offered us security we knew we would never get going home. As I pondered this decision, I went back to my journals where I had recorded Scriptures God used to challenge me. I came across this passage in Esther, where Mordecai challenges the queen, "Who knows but the Lord has brought you to the land for such a time as this?" (paraphrase of Esther 4:14b). When I had heard the preacher speaking on that passage in my home church in Scotland years earlier, I believed that God was saying that to me. My training at Bible college was meant for me to come back and be that person. As I went through my journal, Scripture after Scripture made the right decision clear. We must go home to Scotland.

It was a heart-rending night when we announced our plans to leave the church. Many people cried. But later that night, Morag said to me, "Ian, we know we are doing the right thing."

We turned our backs on the American dream and followed the call of God. God's plan, set into motion by a pagan printer, was fully realized, and our lives changed forever.

♦   ♦   ♦

Ian Leitch, a native Scot, is an evangelist and Bible teacher with the Heralds Trust ministry—traveling extensively in the United Kingdom, North America, Europe, Romania, Haiti, and India. He also pioneered traveling Bible schools called the New Life Seminars. He and his wife, Morag, have one grown son. Ian attended the Undergraduate School 1966–69.

9

A HIGHER
CALLING

◆   ◆   ◆

THE STORY OF
HUGO L. PÉREZ

I walked away from it all. People thought I was crazy.

I was a respected journalist. For five years I worked for
NBC Network News, serving as an associate producer with
their Chicago bureau. My team covered the top stories that
shaped our nation—the school shootings in Paducah, Jones-
boro, and Columbine; the 1996 presidential campaign; the
1997 Midwestern floods. Sometimes, we were the first persons on the scene. When the McCaughey septuplets were
born in Iowa, I broke the story nationally. We were on the
cutting edge.

For me, a guy who started life in Puerto Rico, who
moved to Chicago as a child living with my family of five in
a one-bedroom apartment with a mattress on the floor,
NBC was a dream job. It challenged all my ambition. I
poured twenty years of energy into five years of intense ac-
complishment. I traveled 100,000 miles a year, stayed at the
best hotels, drove the classiest cars, dined in the finest restau-
rants. By almost any definition, I was a success.

When I resigned, my boss was flabbergasted.

It is hard for many people to understand that some things are more important than perks and privilege, that success is not measured by which rung of the corporate ladder your foot is resting on, that life is more than fulfilled ambition.

I came to that realization slowly.

Since I was a little kid I had wanted to be a journalist; it was all I ever wanted to do. Even though I was living that dream to some degree, things weren't working out as I wanted. While my ambition and energy were running down, I was trying to work hard and do my best. I thought by doing so, I could advance and move up in the network. But I ran into roadblock after roadblock. I reached the associate-producer level and could do nothing to get promoted beyond it. I felt as though I was hitting my head against a glass ceiling.

God, I prayed, *You brought me here. You prepared me. You've given me these opportunities. Here I am at the forefront of everything that's going on in this field. Why can't I move forward?*

One very powerful correspondent with whom I worked blocked me from three different opportunities for advancement. Each time he took me out to lunch and said, "I'm not letting you get this promotion, because I like the way you work for me, and I don't want to lose you. If you get promoted, you're going to be gone."

Some compliment!

◆　　　◆　　　◆

OK, God, I prayed. *Whether I get promoted or not, I will represent You. I will be Your man here in the media.*

Inspired by the same famous quotation that energized D. L. Moody, "The world has yet to see what God can do with a man who is wholly devoted to Him," I determined to be Christ's ambassador. Like Daniel in the administration of Darius, I wanted to represent Christ well by being neither corrupt nor negligent. I never wanted to give anyone at NBC the opportunity to say, "Pérez is wishy-washy, he's halfhearted, and he doesn't get the job done." I felt I was representing Christianity to those folks.

That was no easy task. In the newsroom, I got a lot of flack for things just because I was a believer. Although I was one of the network's best associate producers, my colleagues weren't shy about expressing their liberal opinions and ganging up against me, "the conservative." They enjoyed throwing my faith in my face.

My faith was an asset to the network in the school-shooting stories. Given that Christians were targeted in those shootings on public school campuses, the world's attention was riveted to people who were modeling a Christian response to death. People were suddenly open to the hope that can be found through Jesus Christ. My bosses recognized that I had a rapport with these people and gave me the opportunity to interview many of the families and friends of the victims. However, that was an exception to the rule.

Most of the time, I was told to park my faith at the door.

I wanted to express my Christian worldview through my work. But my opportunities to integrate my faith and my career were limited. I was just supposed to be *reporting the news.* I seldom could insert my passion for God into these stories.

Since my opportunities for ministry within my job were limited, I wanted to minister outside my job. I wanted to have a meaningful ministry in my local church. But that was impossible. I was on call 24/7, 365 days a year. To cover every important emerging news story, I was pulled out of all sorts of events—birthday parties, days off, dinners, movies—all to cover a story. At one point, I had just rented an apartment and asked for two days off to make the move. I was halfway finished when they called me to go on a story, so I had to drop everything. Unlike local news crews who went out and covered stories and then were finished in a couple of hours, network assignments could last a week, two weeks—nobody ever knew! In fact, we were trained to travel with a prepared suitcase in our cars, so we could leave on a moment's notice. A good example of this was when I covered the floods in South Dakota (a story that earned me an Emmy). I was sent for a weekend, and I didn't come back for three months!

I wasn't able to minister *at all* in my church. I couldn't even attend regularly. I missed fellowshipping with other believers, participating in worship, and serving others. I wanted to be teaching Bible studies, discipling people, and developing closer relationships. I was starving for meaningful interaction with other Christians.

But there was nothing sacred about my personal life. Church commitments didn't matter to my employer. Neither did friendships.

That was the worst part of my job.

To me, much of what is redemptive about Christianity is warm, stable, supportive relationships. Christianity brought me out of my difficult past. My father was an alcoholic. Sober, he was a loving father. Put a couple drinks in him, and he was a different person. Like the transformation from Dr. Jekyll to Mr. Hyde, he turned mean. The family scattered when he came home. My mom took the brunt of his violence, and I was the only person to stand up to him. As his drinking increased, the abuse spiraled out of control.

One day I told my mother, "That's it! I'm kicking him

out of the house. I'm tired of this." I asked my father to leave. To my surprise, he did. It was really abrupt. One day we were a family (albeit dysfunctional); the next day we were a broken home.

I was a young teen when my parents divorced. I struggled to form my identity as a man without a father figure. God remembered me, however. He led me to Inner City Impact (ICI), a ministry for kids in Chicago. There I met Nathan Strand, a missionary with ICI, who became a father figure for me during those latter teenage years. He did much to encourage me and set my feet on solid ground.

At ICI I came to know Christ as my Savior. ICI had a great program of follow-up, so within a week I was enrolled in an intensive discipleship program. For the next four years, I grew and developed deep relationships with other believers. During that time, I also became a member of the church that I still attend, Good News Bible Church. Through this local body, I was able to develop friendships that have really encouraged me in the good times and tough times.

But now, with my work schedule, how could I be a friend to anyone? I never knew when my pager would go off. I set dates but couldn't keep them. Any appointment on my personal calendar could be slashed at any time. I really couldn't have friends, but I needed strong friendships, since I was working in a field that some called "the den of thieves," where little spiritual light was present. However, I didn't have those vibrant relationships during those five years. I was on my own. I was starving; I needed Christian fellowship in my life.

I remember the moment when I decided it was time to leave my job with NBC. It was a Fourth of July weekend. Six months earlier I had scheduled to have the day off and arranged to have about fifteen friends over to my house for a barbecue. It had been a long time since I had been able to spend a day with them. Shortly into this gathering, a major news story broke and I got paged. The minute my pager rang, I had tears in my eyes. When I called in, my boss told me that I had a half hour to get on the road. I begged and I pleaded, but it didn't do any good. He said, "Well, you have a choice—either get on the road or you don't have to come in again." I had to leave my friends and quickly get on the road.

The inner turmoil wasn't worth it any longer. When the Fourth of July story was wrapped up, I went in and talked with my boss.

When I turned in my resignation, my boss was completely floored. I was someone he had grown to count on. I was the guy in my bureau that they usually called on first for assignments. My bosses, who weren't believers, questioned my decision to leave, saying, "Doesn't God take care of you here? Why can't God use you here?" Although I left on good terms, they couldn't understand my need to be in ministry service and have deep relationships.

I walked away.

◆   ◆   ◆

Yes, at times I miss my job. The summer after I left, the Elían Gonzalez immigration and custody story broke. I thought to myself, *That would have been me there with my team!* The same thoughts crossed my mind during the Florida election scandal in 2000 and the terrorist attacks on September 11. *Here I am away from it all. Did I miss an opportunity to represent God in these areas?*

I have had second thoughts and misgivings. *Should I*

have left the network? Did God really lead me in a new direction, or did I jump the gun? Was I too ambitious while working there, and did I lose sight of the platform God had given me? If I had been more patient, would I have obtained the promotion I desired and, with it, a better schedule? Could I have done something different and made it work?

Some of these questions may go unanswered until I get to heaven. But I am clear that God wanted me to step away from the NBC job and let it go. It was driving me, and I had little control over my life.

It took courage to walk away. But I needed to fan the flame of my faith and set my professional interests aside. Making ambition and accomplishments my identity did not fulfill me. I needed to pursue God in the same way He was pursuing me. When I walked away, I felt a tremendous weight lifted off my shoulders. There were more important things in my life to pursue. Since I left, my relationships have grown and my ministry at the church has been fruitful. God didn't pull me away without a purpose.

Will I return to journalism? I don't know. The dream hasn't died. But right now, it is in God's hands. God is good. He opens doors we never thought possible. And, if He closes them, He is only showing us a better way.

◆　　　◆　　　◆

Hugo Pérez is now the director of communications at the American Heart Association in Chicago. He is actively involved in his church as church chairman, deacon, and "shepherd" to young adults. He also teaches journalism part-time at Chicago's Columbia College. He attended the Undergraduate School 1989–92.

10

CARROT CAKE AND ROMANS 8:28

◆   ◆   ◆

THE STORY OF
RUTH SENTER

I looked up at the ceiling of the hospital and said, "Three strikes and You're out, God. This isn't funny anymore. I don't like what You're doing."

I felt betrayed.

All my life, I tried to obey God. *And what do I get in return for my obedience?*

◆   ◆   ◆

Strike one. I was driving home from church one lovely October day. The driver of a gas truck missed a stop sign and ran right through the intersection, hitting me. It all happened so fast that I had no chance to avoid the accident. The impact of the truck crushed my car. I survived the accident with minor back injuries. Nothing major; I went away singing, "God is so good."

Strike two. In November my gynecologist said, "Your mammogram shows a mass in your left breast." Exploratory surgery was necessary. The reports came back; the lump was benign. So, I was still singing, "God is so good."

Strike three. Three months later, on a cold, snowy February day, the children took the toboggan off the wall in the garage and said, "Let's go to the forest preserve and toboggan." So we spent the afternoon tobogganing. I stood at the top of the hill and watched them because I was nursing the sore back from my car accident in October. I could still feel the aftereffects of the accident—it felt like porcupine quills going up and down my back. It wasn't major pain, just discomfort.

On the last run of the day, the children said, "C'mon, Mom!" I decided at that moment that I didn't want to grow old standing at the top of the hill watching my kids have fun. My husband was already on the toboggan with the children, and I plopped down with them. With four of us on the toboggan, we started downhill. Instead of going down the ramp and gliding onto the frozen lake, our weight threw us off course. We cut our own path down the hill. At the bottom, we dropped onto the lake with a great deal of force. The abrupt landing broke my back.

I was in the hospital for fourteen days. Then I returned home to recover from the fracture of my L1 vertebrae. That meant I needed to stay flat on my back for two more months.

I went home, and pain went home with me. I didn't know what to do with all the pain. I couldn't think straight. It was a constant distraction. I couldn't concentrate on anything or anybody but the pain. It was as though I was locked inside myself and couldn't get beyond myself. Physical pain gave way to emotional and spiritual pain.

God let me down. He has hurt me. Look at all I've done for

Him. What is He doing to me? There was no room in my thoughts to remember God's faithfulness in the past. My charmed life was over. In the past, the Lord had always parted the waters as He did with the Red Sea and allowed me to live a golden life. I grew up as one girl among four boys—always the queen bee. I had a great marriage and two wonderful children. My personality earned me lots of friends. I had five books in print and had published a number of magazine articles. My husband, Mark, was developing a dynamic youth ministry. In the past, God was good. Now, He had let me down. And feeling let down by God was devastating.

Gone was my ability to control anything. I couldn't control what we were having for dinner. I couldn't control what my kids were doing, wearing, or where they were going. I couldn't perform the functions that I had always performed as a mother.

Instead, I was being mothered and cared for by other people—my mother, my husband, my children, my friends, my church. In the past, my strong personality drove my accomplishments. Whatever I determined to do—I was able to do. But now I could not *do* anything. Everybody else did everything for me.

I hated it. I resented people coming into my bedroom, cleaning my bathrooms, and bringing in food. I finally had a dear friend point out to me, "You really have a hard time letting people help you, don't you? You're usually the one bringing the casseroles."

Wrapped in the cocoon of my own suffering, I distanced myself from God, from family, and from friends. I didn't pray, except to say, *You are going to do what You want with me anyway, so it doesn't matter what I do.* I didn't know what my children were doing in school. I didn't talk to Mark about what was happening in his ministry. I didn't want anybody interrupting my self-imposed isolation.

By God's grace, my husband and my children were very patient. The kids came to my room, where we had dinner on my bed every night. Mark brought up a big tray. They all lined up at the foot of my bed, bringing papers from school, and just kept talking to me. Mark told me what was happening at church. Their persistent love was present even though I wasn't listening. I was so consumed with my own misery that I literally couldn't get out of myself.

◆　　　◆　　　◆

One Sunday morning, Mark and the children went off to church and left the radio playing. A preacher came on and had the nerve to start speaking on Romans 8:28 (NIV), "And we know that in all things God works for the good of those who love him, who have been called according to his purpose." I wasn't in any mood for a radio preacher! I especially wasn't in any mood for a radio preacher to talk to me about Romans 8:28, because good things were not happening to me. *The car accident, the benign tumor, the toboggan accident —how could you call that good?*

But it hurt too much to get out of bed and turn the radio off. So I lay there and listened to what he had to say. I have no idea who this preacher was, but he told a story that God used to change my life.

The day before he preached this sermon, his wife was baking in the kitchen. She was making a carrot cake from scratch. He walked into the kitchen and looked at the cake ingredients. Every one of those ingredients, by itself, would taste awful— flour, salt, baking powder, baking soda. Even sugar, though a spoonful of sugar makes the medicine go down, is not something you eat by the spoonful. Almost everything she put in, except the carrots, was awful all by itself.

But the outcome was very different than the ingredients. The preacher said, "I went away and came back forty-five minutes later. Then I smelled the appetizing aroma. Minutes later, I sank my teeth into moist, lush, delicious carrot cake.

"This," he said, "is what Romans 8:28 is all about! Each ingredient of our lives, by itself, may be distasteful. It may be painful. We may wish to spit it out.

"But," he added, "I'm here to tell you that God is making carrot cake out of your life. So, no matter what your bed of affliction, or no matter what the hardship you're facing, it's going to produce carrot cake."

The tears flowed as my heart softened.

I had misunderstood the blessings of God. I had been complaining about the ingredients. His mind was on the cake. On that Sunday morning, flat on my back with the radio on, I realized for the first time that God's grace includes the good and the bad.

In the past, I had lived in a fantasy world where God's blessings meant things went my way. Now I discovered that pain is part of God's love. That is a difficult concept, one I continue to grapple with.

So, I prayed, with a softened heart, *Your love for me can include pain.*

This paradigm shift made it easier to accept help from other people. Being needy is a humbling experience, but it was where God wanted me to be. This was another part of the carrot-cake lesson, this humbling that I felt was an opportunity to learn to allow people to come around me in my time of need and do for me. Allowing this opened me up to God's love, because then I could receive it.

My life up to this point had been so much about *doing*. Doing, and doing well, defined me. I was a perfectionist. I let perfectionism drive me and pressure everyone around me. I had to be the perfect homemaker, the perfect wife, the perfect writer, the perfect mother. My perfectionism once put me in the hospital emergency room. I had been furiously typing on a book manuscript, trying to get it right, when I collapsed in exhaustion.

The doctor said, "What have you been doing?"

I said, "I haven't been doing anything really, just trying to finish up a book project."

He replied, "Put it away. Don't look at it for three weeks. Stop!"

But I said, "I'm already two months late. I can't put it away."

He said, "Put it away!" He gave me something to calm me down and sent me home to rest. That was the result of my perfectionism.

But now, my back was broken. The journey through this pain and weakness made me realize that I was broken in other places as well. I wanted God to heal my back. But He was also busy healing my need to be perfect.

A powerful lesson from my childhood came back to me with fresh meaning.

◆   ◆   ◆

My brain-damaged brother was eighteen months older than I. Growing up, I knew early on that Jimmy was different, but I didn't understand why. I got impatient with him because he never could catch on to what I wanted him to do when we were playing. However, no matter how I treated him, he was the most loving-hearted person I ever met. As a six-year-old, this grated on me; it bugged me that he was so kind.

One day, I was overwhelmed with my sin and the contrast between Jimmy's kindness and my impatience. I went to my mother and asked, "Why is Jimmy so nice?"

She smiled. "Jimmy has asked Jesus to come into his life and help him be kind. Jimmy has a helper, and that helper is Jesus."

I went away and sat on a log out on the edge of the woods. I thought about it for a while and decided I needed a helper to make me nicer and kinder. When I told my mother, she took her Bible and pointed me to verses of Scripture that talked about God loving me, and it suddenly clicked that Jimmy was kind of like God. Jimmy loved me no matter what I did. That's how God loved me, no matter how bad I was.

God used that to bring me to Himself. I was born again that day thanks to Jimmy's Christlike example.

◆   ◆   ◆

I could no longer be the perfect mother, the perfect writer, the perfect wife, the perfect anything. But God still loved me, even though I was incapable of pleasing Him with my "perfection."

As long as I was *doing*, I was in control. Now I could not *do*, and I had no control.

Suddenly I understood that I was never really in control. Somebody else is in charge of my life.

◆　　　◆　　　◆

Our mind is on the ingredients; God's mind is on the carrot cake. God sent a vine to shade Jonah from the hot desert sun. Jonah was happy. God sent a worm to eat the vine. Jonah was angry. Should I accept the vine from God and not the worm?

God is ultimately in charge. What comes into my life—the good and the bad—comes under the umbrella of the sovereignty of God. Understanding this defines my life and gives me the ability to talk to people where they really live.

The brokenness I experienced changed the way I write, it changed the way I deal with people, and it brought realism to my life and a proper understanding of what God's blessings mean. I approach life now with a clear awareness of my own vulnerability. I write and I teach more realistically, because the fantasy world is gone. I serve in our church as director of women's ministries. I love the work. I love the women. Many of them have deep hurts. Many of them are broken just like I am. I understand now that brokenness is everywhere. Others are broken just as I am. God is fixing our broken places, and He uses His Word and other people in that process.

Ernest Hemingway once said, "Sooner or later life breaks most everyone, but some are strong in the broken places." This rang true for me, because the strongest place in my back today is my L1 vertebrae, where my back was broken. And the strongest places in my life are the places where I've come to God and said, "I'm broken in this area and I need You to mend me." As I open myself up to His Word and to the counsel of others, growth happens and I am healed.

God doesn't owe me anything. Everything that I receive

from Him, the good and the bad, is a gift of grace. When I don't expect anything from Him, then I'm thankful for everything He gives me. Coming to grips with brokenness helps me live a thankful life. I truly believe that. I'm not perfect, but God, by His grace, is teaching me.

◆   ◆   ◆

Ruth (Hollinger) Senter *has written eleven books and has contributed to magazines such as* The Christian Reader, Decision, Christian Life, Moody, Christianity Today, *and* Discipleship Journal. *Her husband, Mark, is a professor at Trinity Evangelical Divinity School (Illinois). They have two grown children. Ruth attended the Undergraduate School 1962–65.*

MAY GOD BE GLORIFIED
... BY LIFE OR BY DEATH

◆ ◆ ◆

THE STORY OF
JOHN   AND   BETTY   STAM

Seven hundred college students rose to their feet to say yes to God. They knew the cost of their decision. For some it would mean giving up the hope of marriage. For some it would mean deprivation far away from American comforts. For some it might even mean death.

The scene was a January 1935 chapel service at Moody Bible Institute. These students had just processed the terrible news that a few weeks earlier, two of "their own," recent graduates John and Betty (Scott) Stam, had been martyred for their faith by Communist guerillas in China.

The Communists struck down two soldiers of the Cross. But, in the place of the fallen, an army rose up to take the Gospel to the ends of the earth. Though their lives were cut short, John and Betty Stam left their mark for eternity.

The students who rose to their feet realized these martyrs were ordinary people who gave their lives to an extraordinary God.

◆ ◆ ◆

John grew up in New Jersey, the son of a Christian businessman. But he did not, at first, embrace the faith of his parents. While his parents were occupied with a street-mission ministry in New Jersey, John was busy trying to acquire wealth in New York City. He was once heard saying "he would do anything, run a mile out of his way, if necessary, to avoid being seen at or near one of the Mission's street meetings."[1]

But, in 1923, the Lord used a blind evangelist to bring John to Christ. Then God called him to full-time ministry. In September 1929, he took the savings he had acquired from his business career and used the funds to enroll at Moody Bible Institute.

At Moody, John overcame a less-than-stellar academic history and progressed toward Christian maturity. A diary entry reflects that growth:

> I have been thinking that our God never gives us too many lessons at once. While I am . . . learning to trust Him alone—God grant that I may learn it fully—last term I had some severe struggles and lessons in self-denial. I remember promising the Lord that I would deny myself after refusing to pass out tracts. What misery I had, when I did not want to deny myself for His sake. God grant that the lesson is learned, but I fear I have further installments still to come. "Fear" did I write? "His way is perfect—He will make my way perfect."[2]

Moody afforded John with his first cross-cultural ministry experience. For more than a year, he traveled two hundred miles each way most weekends to minister to a small congregation in Elida, Ohio. This rural church surrounded by farmland was an enormous contrast to his urban upbringing. It tested his ability to cross cultures and minister. He passed the test.

◆   ◆   ◆

Meanwhile, in another part of the world, Betty Alden Scott, the oldest of five children, grew up in Shantung Province in China where her parents were missionaries. Betty's father, Dr. Charles Scott, had left a distinguished university career in the United States to pursue God's work overseas. After attending boarding school near Beijing, Betty enrolled at Wilson College in Pennsylvania.

Betty chose the words of Paul as her life motto: "For to me to live is Christ, and to die is gain" (Philippians 1:21 KJV). She chose this after a powerful encounter with God during a summer conference at Keswick in New Jersey. She wrote:

> Keswick is over, but I trust never the message! Thank the Lord! I have now surrendered myself to the Lord more than I ever realized was possible. . . . I don't know what God has in store for me. I really am willing to be an old-maid missionary, or an old-maid anything else, all my life, if God wants me to. It's as clear as daylight to me that the only worth-while life is one of unconditional surrender to God's will, and of living His way, trusting His love and guidance.[3]

As an outgrowth of this surrender, she began seeking to learn God's plan for her life. As she prayed through this, she felt compelled to return to China as a missionary. After graduating from Wilson *magna cum laude,* Betty enrolled at Moody Bible Institute in 1928 to obtain practical missions training.

In Betty's first year at Moody, she wrote additional stanzas to a hymn entitled "Open My Eyes," which revealed the way God was preparing her heart for missions work.

Open my eyes, that I may see
This one and that one needing Thee,
Hearts that are dumb, unsatisfied,
Lives that are dead, for whom Christ died.

Open my eyes in sympathy,
Clear into man's deep soul to see;
Wise with Thy wisdom to discern,
And with Thy heart to love to yearn.

Open my eyes in power, I pray,
Give me the strength to speak today,
Some one to bring, dear Lord, to Thee,
Use me, O Lord, use even me![4]

While students at Moody, John and Betty met as a result
of the home ministry of Dr. and Mrs. Isaac Page, who were
Chicago-area representatives with China Inland Mission
(now known as Overseas Missions Fellowship). Each week
students gathered at the Pages' home to learn more about
China and pray for the people who needed Jesus.

During China's Boxer Rebellion, around 1900, adver-
saries to the Gospel had claimed the lives of 135 missionaries
and 53 of their children. Many more Christians were killed
as the Communist influence spread in China following
World War I. Despite these losses, the church of Jesus Christ
was growing, and China Inland Mission launched a campaign called the Forward Movement to send two hundred
new missionaries to meet the ministry need. Betty's poem
"The Two Hundred-Forward" captured the heart of this
campaign.

We follow His train —
The bright Morning Star.
He led o'er the seas
From countries afar.
He gently says "Come!"
He supplies all our needs;
So,—Forward, Two Hundred!
'Tis Jesus Who leads![5]

The needs in China gnawed at John and Betty's hearts. John wrote to his brother and said, "A million a month pass into Christless graves over there."[6] The great spiritual need in China drove their desire to reach the unreached. The eternal destiny of the Chinese people depended on missionaries like them.

This was no easy decision. They knew that captivity or death was the price they might have to pay for the sake of the Gospel. But the Lord seemed to be leading John and Betty to China. They started to grow together as a result of this common interest. But it was too soon to know for sure if marriage was God's plan. Neither wanted to sacrifice God's call on his or her life if the other was not meant to be in China.

Betty was a year ahead of John in school and was accepted by China Inland Mission to be a missionary, so they decided to delay their engagement until they had clear direction from the Lord that He was leading John to China as well. The decision for them to wait to marry was difficult. About this same time, John heard of a former student who seemed to have gotten out of the will of God as a result of dropping out of school to get married. He didn't want his interest in Betty to short circuit what God had planned for them individually. In John's diary, he wrote about this struggle.

Betty is in Philadelphia now, but I have not been able to write her a letter. After much searching of my heart and of the Scriptures, I feel that the Lord would be displeased at my going forward in this direction. . . . And now that Betty and I are looking forward to the same field, I cannot move one step closer in her direction until I am sure that it is the Lord's directive will. I don't want to wreck her life and mine too.[7]

The wait was agonizing, but the Lord used this time of separation to cement their relationship and common call to China.

As his senior year at Moody was coming to a close, John was chosen from among his peers as class speaker for his graduation in 1932. He challenged those present with these words:

Shall we beat a retreat, and turn back from our high calling in Christ Jesus, or dare we advance at God's command in face of the impossible? . . . Let us remind ourselves that the Great Commission was never qualified by clauses calling for advance only if funds were plentiful and no hardship or self-denial involved. On the contrary, we are told to expect tribulation and even persecution, but with it victory in Christ.[8]

That same year, as Betty was completing her first year with China Inland Mission, John was accepted to that mission board. John immediately sent Betty a letter from Philadelphia, asking the long-awaited question, "Will you marry me?"

John had no time to wait for a reply before he began his journey across the Pacific aboard the ship *Empress of Japan*. Crossing the ocean seemed to take forever, because the answer to John's proposal was still unknown. In God's providence, Betty came down with tonsillitis and was delayed in Shanghai, the port where the *Empress of Japan* was due to arrive. At that unexpected reunion, Betty accepted John's offer of marriage. The China director gave his permission for them to marry as soon as John had completed his first year on the field.

John and Betty departed from Shanghai and did not see each other again until the evening before their wedding. They were assigned to different areas of China, John in southeastern Anhwei and Betty in northwest Anhwei.

In preparation for their wedding, Betty wrote the following sonnet about "the ring."

> Dearest, when thou desirest to buy a ring,—
> Sweetheart, in this obey me without fail;
> Give me no diamond which is for sale—
> It is too glittering, too cold a thing.
> Buy me no platinum; I cannot sing
> Of such a metal, precious, but too pale!
> And bandits' robbing soon would end the tale.
> Thy love is more than ransom for a king.
> It is enough that I should have thy heart.
> And when thou tak'st me, Lover, for thy bride,
> Give me a ring of gold, not thick or wide,
> Pure gold like thee, God's finest work of art.
> I also thought; into the Heavens new,
> Where streets are gold, I might take thy ring, too.[9]

On October 25, 1933, John and Betty were married open-air style at her family's home in Tsinan. It was a beautiful day and a joyous occasion. Their honeymoon was spent in Betty's childhood town of Tsingtao. The exuberance of finally being married was more than they could imagine. Two days after they exchanged vows, John wrote to his family:

> This letter is from your newly married couple at Tsingtao. Oh, the Lord has been so good in all the arrangements that we are just praising Him all along the way! We are having a blessed time together, and there is so much to tell you about that I am going to see if I cannot lay violent hands on some typewriter around here, before our blessings pile up so high that I may forget some of them.[10]

At the end of their honeymoon, John spoke of the beautiful day they had experienced aboard a sailing vessel, but noted "the only fly in the ointment was that I didn't speak to anyone aboard about his soul."[11]

On September 11, 1934, a baby girl, Helen Priscilla, was born to the couple. John's comments capture the delight they shared over this beautiful gift from God: "But you should see our daughter! She really is the cutest thing . . . and would do for any baby show, as far as good looks is concerned, right now.[12]

Shortly after Helen's birth, the Stams moved ministry locations because of the recent escalation of banditry and thieving in Miaosheo. Communist bandits, intent on extinguishing the church of Jesus Christ, broke into homes and robbed people of their possessions. American missionaries were especially vulnerable because the Communists wanted to rid China of Christians through intimidation. The hatred for Christian missionaries was fueled by conspiracy theories spread to discredit their motivations and methods.

The Stams moved into a home in Tsingteh. The district magistrate assured them, "There is no danger of Communists here. I will guarantee your safety." But a few weeks later, when news came of approaching Communist soldiers, this official was one of the first to flee.[13] John and Betty had been married for just over a year when John received the report that the Communists were coming. There was no time to leave. There was no time to hide.

The Communists forced their way into the Stam home. John and Betty greeted them with kindness. While John was talking with the leaders, trying to provide their demands for goods and money, Betty prepared tea and cakes for them. At the conclusion of the visit, the Stam family was taken captive. Ransom was demanded. On December 6, 1934, John wrote to the China Inland Mission center in Shanghai, stating the Communist demands.

Dear Brethren,

My wife, baby and myself are today in the hands of the Communists, in the city of Tsingteh. Their demand is twenty thousand dollars for our release.

All our possessions and stores are in their hands but we praise God for peace in our hearts and a meal tonight. God grant you wisdom in what you do, and us fortitude, courage and peace of heart. He is able, and a wonderful friend in such a time.

Things happened so quickly this A.M. They were in the city just a few hours after the ever-persistent rumors really became alarming, so that we could not prepare to leave in time. We were just too late.

The Lord bless you and guide you. As for us—may God be glorified, whether by life or by death.

In Him,
John C. Stam[14]

But ransom arrangements were never made. Instead, two days later, on December 8, 1934, at ten o'clock in the morning, the Communists stripped John and Betty of their outer clothes, bound them painfully, marched them through the town of Miaosheo, shouting ridicule and calling the townspeople to the execution. They forced them to kneel on the side of the road in a pine grove on top of a hill outside the city.

John leaned over to Betty and spoke words that only she could hear while an executioner stood behind them with sword in hand. Together they knelt on the threshold of eternity. They had considered this scenario many times before, but now possibility converged with reality.

The sword flashed, and John's body collapsed to the ground. Betty trembled, and quickly the sweep of the sword reached her and took her life. "The two who had been parted for an instant, were united in the presence of the Lord."[15]

By God's grace, Helen Priscilla's life was spared. After John and Betty were taken captive, their baby was placed in a vacant house and was found a day later by a Chinese evangelist seeking her whereabouts. The baby had gone that entire time without food or care. The pastor eluded the Communists and carried the baby a hundred miles in a rice basket. Along the way, he found a nursing mother to temporarily care for Helen, and then he went to great lengths to take her to a hospital for observation. Eventually, Betty's parents were located, and they cared for Helen as their own child.

"The blood of the martyrs is the seed of the church."[16] After American missionaries were slaughtered during the Boxer Rebellion, twice as many missionaries replaced those who had been killed. American missionaries and countless thousands of Chinese believers met their deaths at the hands of the Communists, but today the Chinese church numbers in the tens of millions.

The deaths of John and Betty Stam brought those seven hundred Bible college students to their feet on that cold January day in 1935. Hundreds committed their lives to a deeper walk with Christ and yielded themselves to serving God wherever He may take them.

God was glorified in the Stams, in life and in death.

◆   ◆   ◆

*John Stam was born in 1907, and **Elisabeth Alden Scott** was born in 1906; both were killed December 8, 1934. Betty attended Moody's Undergraduate School 1928–31, and John attended 1929–32.*

12

PRAYING
PIONEER

· · ·

THE STORY OF
GEORGE VERWER

The KGB officer in charge of my interrogation said I was a spy. "We have a place for American spies," he told me. *Oh, no,* I thought. *They're offering me an all-expense-paid trip to Siberia.*

Things were not going well. The Soviets had our vehicle. They were interrogating my partner, Roger, in another room. It was just a matter of time before they would discover the Bibles and the printing press we had smuggled into the heart of the Communist empire.

It was 1961. The Cold War was in full swing. My dream of taking the Gospel into closed countries—not to mention my life—could come to a very quick end. *What to do?*

· · ·

Anybody who knew me wouldn't be surprised at the predicament I was in. People called me a radical. Ever since my 1955 conversion at a Billy Graham meeting in New York City, I was always diving headfirst into any opportunity I could find to share the Gospel. Soon after I was saved, I got a chance to speak to the entire student body of my high school, and I used it to talk about Jesus. I shared my faith door-to-door. I organized rallies—600 people came to one of them, and 125 stood up to make decisions for Christ (including my own father). In 1957 I arranged to get people to the Billy Graham crusade, literally by the busload. But I did not attend the crusade myself. Since every seat was taken, I did not want to take a seat in the crusade that could be occupied by a non-Christian. So, while Billy Graham preached in Madison Square Garden, I went out into the streets of New York City and preached. Then, with two friends, I took off to evangelize Mexico.

It just made sense. *Why not go someplace where people haven't heard the Gospel?*

In those days, Mexico was a semiclosed country. Protestants were persecuted. Importing Christian literature was illegal. Our car was full of it; my friends and I had no idea how we were going to get across the border.

But we got across. We prayed much, stuffed our literature under our mattresses, crossed the border at night, and the guards waved us through.

We worked among people living in the garbage dumps. The enormous poverty gripped me. As I watched flies crawling across the eyes of little babies, my heart cried out to God, *What can I do to awaken this nation to the life-changing Gospel of Jesus Christ?*

Radio. We decided to get on the radio. There was only one problem. In Mexico, Christian radio was illegal. *There's got to be a way around this!*

I came back to the USA, transferred from my liberal arts college to Moody Bible Institute, organized a team of five, and headed back to Mexico. Before we left we prayed. When we got to Mexico, God gave us a plan. We started a bookstore. Then we went to the radio station.

"We represent a bookstore. We want to advertise. We sell Bibles. The reason people don't buy the Bible is that they don't know what's in it. We'd like to read from it in our advertisement."

It worked. We read and explained the Scriptures over Mexican radio. That was the beginning of a weekly, fifteen-minute program.

◆　　　◆　　　◆

Back at Moody, I prayed, I planned, I organized, and I read missionary books. I dreamed about getting into countries like Iraq and Afghanistan. Hardly any Christians were there —*it's the perfect opportunity!*

I didn't want romance to derail me, so I went on what I called a social fast—no dating—and that lasted for two years. But one day I met a Wisconsin farm girl named Drena.

My social fast ended immediately. I was in love.

But I wanted to make sure that Drena shared my radical commitment to world missions. On our first date I said to her, "Probably nothing is going to happen between you and me, but I'm going to be a missionary, and if you marry me, you'll probably end up being eaten by cannibals in New Guinea."

She was definitely not in love with me.

I persisted. Eventually, we got engaged. I never wanted to spend any money, because I wanted every dime to go to spreading the Gospel. *Why buy meals when Moody provides them?* was my mind-set. Yet one day, at mealtime, we were on a date, sitting by Lake Michigan. I often skipped meals, but I didn't think it was right to ask her to skip a meal, so I asked the Lord if He would somehow supply food for her without our spending any money. The people sitting behind us were having a picnic, and they packed up and left. I went to the wastebasket, pulled out the brown paper bag they had discarded, and discovered a sandwich that was not even unwrapped. I gave it to my fiancée. She got a real taste of what she was getting married to!

We were married in Milwaukee in 1960 just after I graduated.[1] At the time, I hardly believed in marriage ceremonies, so we had our wedding during the Sunday morning church service so the pastor could preach the Gospel to the non-Christians present. During the reception, my close friend Dale Rhoton stood up and said, "The main thing you can give to George and Drena is prayer, because they're selling everything else for the sake of the Gospel."[2]

We skipped the honeymoon and went straight to Mexico. On our way, we decided not to spend any money. The first night we took our wedding cake to a gas station in Wheaton, Illinois, offering to barter. They filled the tank and let me keep the cake. The next morning, another station owner—a Christian—let me keep the cake too. The next guy was not so generous, but he liked cake. We traded the cake for gas. We got all the way to Mexico without spending a cent.

For six months we opened bookstores and evangelized. Then we moved to another closed country: Spain. Spain, under Franco, had little toleration for the Gospel. So I made it my home base while I studied Russian and prepared to launch into the Soviet Union.

The plan in the Soviet Union was simple. Roger Malstead

and I smuggled in Scripture portions and a printing press. There we planned to look up addresses in the phone book and mail these Gospels to Soviet citizens. Things were going well until I accidentally spilled melted butter on one of the Gospels, rendering it unusable.

"Flush it down the toilet," Roger suggested.

But I hated wasting that Scripture. *I know what to do*, I thought. *I'll find some isolated spot in the countryside where no one can see us, and I'll throw it out the window. Then someone can pick it up and read it!*

That was a mistake. Someone did see us. Within ten miles, we were stopped at a major roadblock and arrested as spies.

They interrogated us for two days. I decided to tell them the truth. When they found out we had a printing press hidden in our car, they freaked out. They grabbed us, dragged us off to our car, stripped the car, and found our printing press and all our other literature.

We were headline news in Soviet Russia. *Pravda* liked the story so much that it reran it ten years later.

At the time of our interrogation, the Russians had just put their first person into outer space. The interrogator said to me, "Look, we've had our spaceman up there, looking around, and we didn't find your God."

I responded by talking my interrogator into singing a hymn.

After two days, they were convinced that we were religious fanatics and not CIA operatives. With a submachine-gun guard, they escorted us out of the country and dropped us in Austria.

My goal, my aim, and my desire was to get the Gospel into closed countries. We had just gone into one of the most closed countries on earth and promptly got kicked out. *What is God doing?* I wondered.

I decided it was time to pray. I climbed a tree in the mountains of Austria to get alone so I could pray. I spent the day in prayer.

That day revolutionized my life and my ministry.

God showed me that my vision was too small. He showed me that my job was to mobilize the church, and He wanted me to start with the European church. It just made sense. Europeans can drive to all kinds of closed countries. Americans, on the other hand, need to cross the Atlantic before they can get to most of the countries we wanted to reach. The amount of money needed to get one American into a closed country could get two or three Europeans into the same place. Even after they got there, Europeans were usually better received than Americans.

Little did I know that this was to be the forerunner of the whole radical change that was to take place in mission thinking. This concept exploded from Europe to Asia to Africa to Latin America. People from all different countries became equal partners in missions.

God gave me a name—the name that has stuck like glue to our movement ever since: *Operation Mobilization (OM)*.

God also showed me how to mobilize the church: Bring people together for a summer, for a year, for two years, and send them on outreaches. Then send them back to their home churches or to another mission agency to energize, re-vitalize the church, and spread the vision.

That was 1961. Short-term missions trips were virtually unheard of. It was a revolutionary concept. But it worked.

The first summer we recruited two hundred volunteers. By the second summer, our group had grown to two thousand, capable of reaching 25 million people. I moved to London, where we assembled a fleet of 120 old trucks. We crossed the English Channel, split up into teams, and drove out to reach the unreached. Within a year of my arrest in the Soviet Union, we were sending the USSR Europeans who spoke fluent Russian and could accomplish more than I ever could.

We focused on getting into closed countries. That's why I sent Dale Rhoton over to check out Afghanistan. "While you're in the neighborhood," I said, "you might as well check out Pakistan and India." I honestly didn't expect much to come from it. I knew missionaries were operating in West Pakistan. And I had already met vibrant Christians from India. Since India's strong churches were reaching India, I figured that country didn't need us.

But Dale told me otherwise. "India needs us," he said.

So we sent two teams, about twenty people, to India. They drove the whole way in old trucks, and they encountered all kinds of problems getting there. I felt responsible, especially since I had recruited many of these team members myself. So around late 1963, I flew to India to see how things were going.

That nation shook me up. I traveled around on the train, always evangelizing and giving out tracts. I was blown away by the needs of the Indian people.

I said to my wife, "We are moving to India."

We moved to Bombay. The people were drawn to our radical message about discipleship, forsaking all, world missions, and prayer. Rather than feeling as though we needed to import a foreign missionary every time we wanted to get something done, we partnered with the church in India and supported nationals in ministry.

Our work exploded with growth, and I got kicked out of the country.

So we moved to Katmandu, Nepal, because there the people of India could come to us without a visa.

◆   ◆   ◆

Logistics was becoming a challenge. Driving old trucks back and forth across Europe and Asia wasn't working quite as well as I wanted it to. As I prayed about this and looked at the globe, I was struck with how much water there is on the surface of the earth.

Then it came to me. *We need a ship!*

This was something new in the Christian world. When I discussed the idea with the churches in Europe, some laughed. To some, owning a ship seemed like a hopeless extravagance.

But the more I prayed about it, the more I was convinced that God wanted us to own a ship. I wanted a ship. I wanted it as soon as possible. Impatience, admittedly, is one of my failings, and God deals with it by making me wait for things. He taught me to wait for six long years before our first ship, the 2,319-ton *Logos I,* set sail in 1971 from England to India.

In those days we didn't believe in fund-raising. We thought we should follow the example of Hudson Taylor and George Müeller—never make our needs publicly known, but privately pray and wait for God to supply. When we signed a contract to purchase the *Umanak* (which became the *Logos I*), we had enough money to make a deposit but not enough to complete the purchase. We prayed, God supplied, and by our deadline we had exactly enough to complete the purchase and have the ship towed to dry dock where it could be overhauled and painted. In recent years, we have come to believe that we should show our esteem for our partners in the local church by sharing our needs with them so they can join us in prayer and in giving.

Though it was exciting to finally have our ship, once we had it, the full reality of it began to sink in. In fact, we nearly shook with fear when we realized the dangers of the ship project—an old vessel, no insurance, all those young people aboard with their parents hovering anxiously in the background. I used to have nightmares about the ship going down, and I would wake up thinking, *Let's keep it in the warmer climates, so that if it does sink at least the kids will have a chance. If you go down in cold seas, there's far less hope.*[3]

Despite our anxieties, the ship ministry became more than we ever expected. We acquired a second, larger ship (the *Doulos*), and they became floating bookstores and literature centers, as well as launching pads for short-term missions. Staffed by four hundred volunteers from forty to fifty nations, our ships visit ports all over the globe from India to Jamaica, from Egypt to Communist China.

Operation Mobilization has grown to three thousand full-time staff plus another three to four thousand short-term missionaries. One hundred thousand people have been trained in OM, representing a wide range of denominations. More than one hundred mission agencies trace their births to their founders or leaders being in OM. One of our literature ministries, Send the Light (STL), is now a separate company with six hundred employees and forty bookstores in the UK. We're in ninety countries, including nearly every Muslim nation on the globe. We have become a much more holistic ministry. In the last ten years, we have put flesh and bone on the compassion of Jesus by reaching out to victims of earthquakes, floods, war, and poverty—meeting physical as well as spiritual needs.

This growth has been a direct and exhilarating answer to prayer. No one accomplishes anything without God. And we certainly didn't get into closed countries without much prayer. We've also seen private answers to prayer. My wife's father was killed in World War II. Her stepfather asked her to leave home because he was so anti-Christian. Yet, after twenty-five years of prayer, he came to Christ.

At Moody, we were known as the little group that was always praying. This was back in the late 1950s when praying in small groups was unheard of. Although I'm sure others were birthing this practice of praying in small groups at the same time, this approach has spread all over the world. Now it's part of our culture. In 1958 we started the practice of meeting for a half night in prayer—a practice that has continued for more than forty years.

I believe in and practice prayer. I believe God answers prayer. Yet unanswered—or seemingly unanswered—prayer is one of the great altars upon which God makes true men and women. My life is full of unanswered prayer. Not even 50 percent of my prayers have been answered over the years, not yet at least.[4]

I aim high. I believe in a great and powerful God. When my hopes, dreams, and prayers are not realized, I get discouraged. In fact, all my life I have struggled with discouragement. But I stand on the promises of God. I have determined to never let the sun go down on my discouragement.

That can be a challenge. We have certainly faced difficult times. For example, just before midnight on January 4, 1988, the *Logos I* struck a rock in the Beagle Channel at the tip of South America. All 139 persons aboard (including a six-month-old baby) were evacuated, and the ship went down. On the evening of August 10, 1991, two young OM missionaries were killed when terrorists threw a grenade into a meeting we were holding in Zamboanga in the Philippines. An OM missionary was kidnapped by Afghans and never heard from again. Another worker was shot in Turkey.

I don't know why these things happened. There is a mystery in suffering that we will never fully understand.

♦   ♦   ♦

I'm not the same person I was in 1960. Yes, I am still eager to share the Gospel. But God has had to change me and change my ideas. Many of us who trained in Bible school back in the 1950s had a Pharisee streak—a grace-killing streak. Our ideas about money, prayer, and evangelism—our man-made rules—became the measuring line of how spiritual people were. We were judgmental. Even when we tried not to be, our body language gave us away.

I was so focused, so zealous, so determined that I used to walk right by people without even acknowledging them. Many times I was too hard on my wife. God confronted me about this, even from the very first month of our marriage when I hurt my wife and I saw her sitting there crying. God used the ministry of men like Oswald J. Smith and Roy Hession to bring me, weeping, back to the Cross.

God showed me that 1 Corinthians 13—the Love Chapter—was, for us, the most important chapter in the Bible. Though I believe in world missions, though I believe in radical commitment, these things mean nothing if we don't have Christ's love.

We need bigheartedness. We need what Charles Swindoll calls a "grace awakening." We need balanced, consistent Christianity.

◆   ◆   ◆

"Missionaries are needed as much as ever," says **George Verwer.** *"Although the percentage of the world's population that has never heard the Gospel has shrunk from 50 percent to 20 percent during my forty-five years of ministry, the number of unreached is still very high."*

Although he will remain involved in literature and related projects reaching one hundred nations, George Verwer plans to turn over the official leadership of Operation Mobilization to his associate director, Peter Maiden, in August 2003.

George Verwer speaks at four hundred meetings a year in churches and other settings all over the globe. He and his wife, Drena, make their home in London, England. Their two sons, one daughter, and five grandchildren are scattered throughout Britain and the United States. George Verwer attended the Undergraduate School 1958–60.

OFFERING HOPE

◆ ◆ ◆

THE STORY OF
TAMARA WHITE

This is it. I'm toast.

The gang leader was walking toward me. Here I was, a young white Kansas woman, wearing a dress, all alone except for the little girl I was with, in the middle of Cabrini Green, one of the most dangerous neighborhoods in Chicago.

"Are you Tammy White?" he asked.

I nodded. *How does he know my name?*

"You're mentoring my cousin," he continued.

"Oh, really?" I said.

"Yeah, I had a tutor when I was a kid."

I started to relax.

"I just want you to know that whenever you're in the Green, you'll always be protected."

◆ ◆ ◆

I came to Chicago to attend Moody Bible Institute to become a foreign missionary. But I found my real calling two blocks away on the streets of Cabrini Green. I fell in love with the people in this neighborhood that was feared and avoided by most of Chicago's millions.

As an organizer of a Big Brother/Big Sister program, I imagined bringing Jesus to that violent neighborhood. But when I got there, I discovered He was already there. He was alive and well, living inside people the rest of the world had forgotten. The women I met who lived in this war zone radiated a faith that transcended anything I had ever experienced.

Most people stay out of Cabrini Green because they don't want to be robbed, raped, or worse. I went in. Though I survived without harm—the gang leader was true to his word—my faith almost did not survive what I experienced.

I wanted to tell these little girls that the love of Jesus would make their lives beautiful. I wanted to tell them that everything would be OK if only they would trust in God. I wanted to say, "Follow Jesus, and He will protect you."

But those sayings didn't stack up to the reality I witnessed.

The Christianity I had grown up with didn't work in the inner city. As I walked into a world of unimaginable suffering, doubts piled high inside. Questions I had never before faced now screamed at me.

If God is so powerful, where is He when His people cry out to Him? If He's so powerful, where is He when these children trust Him and then they are molested that same night? How am I supposed to explain to them who God is and why they should give Him their whole lives when He doesn't protect them? Why would God give man free will when the city overflows with the trouble it has caused?

I really did not have good answers. The well-meaning platitudes of suburban Christianity just did not match what I saw day after day. God does as He pleases, and I couldn't understand why He pleased to let people suffer so.

What kind of God do I serve? Does God, as I know Him, even exist? Or is everything I believe just a clever lie?

But I met people in the inner city who kept the faith, who loved God even though their circumstances were deplorable and they had little hope that those circumstances would change. And I met children and teens who really wanted their lives to be different, who were receptive to Christ.

What do I have to offer them?

My struggle intensified when I saw several of my friends become alienated from other Christians because my friends struggled with the abuse they had endured in their lives.

God, where are You in this? What can we count on You for?

I tried talking with some of my teachers, but the ones I turned to had difficulty understanding what was going on inside me. As I searched for answers, I traveled to Europe and studied at L'Abri. And I talked to many seasoned people who were in ministry. Some of them were honest enough to say they had felt the same way many times, not only in their youth, but also later when they suffered personally. One man served on the mission field for many years only to lose his wife. He struggled with doubt and anger over the goodness of God's intentions.

I was honest with God. I argued with Him. I told Him about my doubts. God honored that honesty.[1] As I revisited the Gospels, He convinced me that there was no one else like Jesus. There was no one else to turn to—whether I understood Him or not, whether I agreed with Him or not. I began to really believe what the Bible teaches: We do live in a fallen world. We're not in heaven yet.

My struggle was not cleanly resolved with pat answers and nice sounding sayings. Instead my thoughts went something like this: *I guess I don't have God by the tail. I cannot make Him do what I want Him to do for hurting people. Sometimes I don't have the answers. God has the answers. But He might not share them with me.*

As I worked my way through these issues, God began showing me that He had designed me to work in the inner city. I love cities. I'm artistic. I'm musical. I love stories. People in inner cities tend to be culturally wired the same way. I have been intrigued with people who struggle with addictions and similar challenges. God had planted inner-city compassion and empathy in me.

After helping to start an inner-city ministry (HOME Ministries) in Chicago, I moved to Denver and started a ministry for homeless teens called Prodigal Coffee House. The volunteer staff and I did not post a sign. We did not buy advertising. We wanted to attract the right people by word of mouth. We prayed that God would enable us to reach gang leaders who would spread the word to others on the street.

We opened the coffeehouse, and no one showed up. That didn't surprise me. Many people just assume that if you provide a service for hurting people, they will come fawning to you. But why would they? These teens are all very wounded. I knew they had no reason to trust me. I knew I had to take the initiative to reach out to them.

When no one showed up, I took to the street to invite people in. As I walked all alone down Colfax Avenue, I came across Beaker, Savage, and Psycho. They were gang leaders, very powerful on the street.

Exactly the people we want to reach, I thought.

I started teasing them. "Come on, guys, when are you going to come to my little coffee shop?"

"All right, all right," they said.

I walked back, made some coffee, and Beaker and Savage showed up. We chatted for about a half hour; then Psycho walked in.

He was furious with me. "Why are you so mad?" I asked him.

He looked at me and said, "Because this is a very dangerous street. I've been looking for you. You shouldn't have walked back by yourself."

There was an immediate connection between the four of us. They trusted me. We felt like we had always known each other. They stayed and drank coffee and told me their stories. They told me how long they had been on the street. (They were fifteen to seventeen at the time.) We sat out on the porch, and they showed me the knives they carried for protection. One of them showed me the pockmarks all over his chest from his mother throwing hot grease on him.

✦　　✦　　✦

About one million teenagers are homeless in America. They roam the country. They live on the streets and sleep under bridges and in abandoned buildings. They jump trains or hitch rides with truckers.

Many people think that these children are runaways, disgruntled boys and girls who get angry with their parents and leave home. In Denver, we see some of those in the summer; the real homeless kids in Denver call them "summer flowers." But the real homeless teens are not runaways. The more appropriate term would be throwaways. In some cases, parents have abandoned them. In other cases, the kids are fleeing incest, abuse, domestic violence. Their parents are satanists, drug dealers, prostitutes, in and out of prison. Some parents are homeless themselves. Some of these kids have never been to school. They live a gypsy existence.

There are public and private services for these kids—mental health, education, housing. But, from their perspective, *why bother?* They have no hope. They are being raped. They are being molested. They are starving. They are invisible. They have every reason to believe that nobody cares whether they live or die. *So why bother?*

•   •   •

That's why I opened Prodigal. We don't provide housing, medical care, or any of a whole array of services already provided by others. Instead, we provide what I call redemptive relationships. Our goal is to be companions to these kids. We believe that if we put volunteers and staff who know Jesus among these kids, we will create a ministry of Christ's presence. Then it's up to God to woo them, to pursue them in the way and at the pace He chooses.

Our job is to listen. We listen to their stories. We listen, and we tell our own stories as well. I tell our volunteers, "Why should they come in and tell you about their father molesting them when you don't tell them anything about you?" Abandonment, addiction, and poverty are difficult for anyone to talk about. We earn their trust by being appropriately honest with them, sharing our struggles as well as our faith.

We don't expect to show up and solve all their problems in a ninety-minute meeting. We understand that redemptive relationships take time and long-term commitment.

The sordid activities that many of these kids are involved

in would make the average churchgoer cringe. We could tell our kids they are sinners, and that would be true. But these kids already know they're sinners. It wouldn't be helpful to them to march in with a message of condemnation before they've had a chance to see we care about them and love them. They've already heard of God's wrath; now they need to know of His love and mercy.

One night, a few months after I met Psycho, he came in and told me he wanted to get some dynamite and blow up the Mile-High Stadium. I asked him why.

"There's a Promise Keepers meeting there. I want to blow up all those *born-agains*," he said.

"But, Psycho," I said, "I'm a born-again."

"No, you're not," he said.

"Yes, I am."

"No, you're not," he insisted.

We went back and forth. Finally, he came behind the counter where I was standing and very gently pushed me up against the wall and started wagging his finger in my face.

"You're not a born-again," he said, "because you don't do this. You don't get in my face like this."

The only Christianity most of these kids know is a religion of condemnation. A nine-year-old boy from our ministry has come to live with me. I hope to adopt him if the legal and custody issues can be worked out. The first week he was with me, I wanted to share with him what a privilege it was to have him in my home. I wanted to tell him how the Bible calls children a gift or reward from God (Psalm 127:3). So I asked him, "Do you know what God says about children?"

He hung his head. "I know," he said. "They are evil."

No matter what age they are, these kids have no trouble

believing in their own depravity. What they struggle with is dignity. How can they interpret their lives from a point of dignity?

Sometimes we spend a weekend with the girls where we talk about sexuality and being a woman of dignity. In their world of prostitution and abuse, we begin to show them who they really are in God's sight.

Some of our teenagers are satanists or survivors of satanic ritual abuse. Others are into wicca or witchcraft.

We occasionally serve Communion as part of a worship service at Prodigal. One time, the son of a satanist mother was present. As we started serving Communion, he quietly got up and left. Later, he came to my office and said, "Can I talk to you?"

"Sure," I said.

"I just wanted to apologize," he said.

"Apologize for what?"

He explained, "I left during Communion, and I know that's very sacred to you. But Mom told me if I was ever in the presence of it, it would destroy me."

So we look for ways to convey Christ to people who have been ostracized by society, ostracized by the church, ostracized by their own terrible experiences.

When we talk about God, we use the language that they give us. Many of these kids went to Sunday school once upon a time. But they weren't able to connect with God. Perhaps no one in the church understood the depth of their suffering, and no one could offer them a Jesus who knows and cares. Whatever the case, we don't feed these kids Christian clichés. We learn their vocabulary and use it.

♦   ♦   ♦

One night some teen boys came to me and said, "Tamara, we think we killed a man last night."

Sometimes teens can be grandiose in their stories. So I listened to what they said. They were high on methamphetamine. So they beat a man down by the river for no other reason than the sheer pleasure of doing it.

Shortly thereafter, they came to a Bible study with a newspaper article describing the crime they committed. The man they had beaten was alive—barely.

"You need to turn yourselves in," I said to them.

I gave them twenty-four hours to turn themselves in or I would. When they came back the next night, I asked them again to turn themselves in. I begged. I pleaded. I started crying in front of everyone.

They just laughed.

So I called the police. All five boys were arrested. The nineteen-year-old was given a long sentence. The father of one of the boys put out a death threat on me, and I needed to move out of my home for three weeks while the police dealt with that.

One of the boys was a sixteen-year-old named Carlos. He was a very tough boy. He was good at avoiding any overtures of love that we tried to give him. He went to prison. As he sat in prison, he hated me with every fiber of his being.

Last summer he was released. Moody students named Josh and Pete were here on an internship. They met Carlos downtown, and they ended up leading him to the Lord.

Then they brought him to my office. We talked for a few minutes about what had happened. Then, right there, he asked for forgiveness. This summer, he was baptized in my church. He is hoping to join a YWAM (Youth With A Mission) six-month discipleship training program, go to Bible school, and become a full-time missionary.

Sure, he struggles with issues from his past. Healing takes time. But if you would have told me years ago that Carlos would be a believer, I would have said, "No way." He was probably one of the few kids I thought, *never.*

♦   ♦   ♦

Psycho was right. Colfax Avenue is a dangerous place. I've been stalked. My life has been threatened. My home has been broken into. I've been punched in the face.

People ask me, "Do you feel safe?"

I do. I feel safe, even though unsafe things have happened. When I lived in Chicago, for example, I was walking down the street one day when I felt the Lord's presence and a sense that I should move away from the curb and closer to the building. As soon as a I did so, a car came tearing around the corner with kids hanging out the window, shooting up the neighborhood with Uzi submachine guns. If I hadn't moved, I would probably be dead.

When I worked in Cabrini Green, the gang leader promised I would be protected. During the next year, on at least three different occasions, someone I didn't know ran up to me in Cabrini Green and said, "You need to leave—*now.*" Each time I left, and minutes later gang warfare broke out on the very spot on which I had been standing.

The summer before I left Chicago, there were twenty murders within a three-block radius of my apartment. The sad thing is, I remember thinking, *They won't kill me. I'm a white woman. My murder would bring the media and the po-*

lice. Those who were murdered were people of color, poor people who "didn't matter" in the eyes of society.

God has protected me. But I also realize that He is under no obligation to spare my life. I could be harmed. I could be killed. It could happen here. But then again, it could happen in the most tame suburban ministry setting.

Not that we don't take precautions. We leave in groups. We have our teens check their weapons at the door. If a teen does bring a gun into the coffeehouse, someone will tell us, and we will politely, but firmly, ask the teen to leave and return without the gun. When we have people from rival gangs in there at the same time, we welcome them. But we explain to them, with respect, "If you're here to start something, then you need to leave."

◆　　　◆　　　◆

Hope is the most dangerous thing we offer these kids. It removes them from the anesthesia of depression, chaos, and survival that they are in. Hope stands in sharp contrast to their world of abandonment, mental illness, addictions, and violence. We can't offer them hope, then take it away. As the Bible says, "Hope deferred makes the heart sick" (Proverbs 13:12).

Hope is deferred a lot for these kids. Yet, without hope, people collapse. We have a delicate balancing act. On one hand, we offer the hope of who Christ is and how He wants to work in our lives. We tell these kids the truth: "You are loved and valuable." But we also have to tell them the other side of the story. "There is no magic pill."

I don't think God is as opposed to suffering as we are. He knows what it brings out in our lives. But I often argue with

Him on this, because I see suffering that I really think He should have done something about.

◆　　　◆　　　◆

For years, before I made that walk down Colfax Avenue, Beaker, Savage, and Psycho had been praying, in their own way, for someone to come and help them. Now that I've been there, now that I've seen God's heart for the poor, it would be impossible for me to walk away.

◆　　　◆　　　◆

"God created Prodigal as much for me as He did for these kids," says **Tamara White.** *"When our volunteers and staff come here, their world is rocked and, their faith is challenged.*

"'How do I explain God to these kids?' we ask ourselves. 'I believe in a God who provides for you and takes care of you, but I can't find anyplace in this kid's life where He's been doing that. How do I speak of God?' Having to wrestle with those kinds of categories—at first it seems like it will crush your faith, but, in the end, it enlarges it. It makes your faith real and deep. This struggle makes you love God for who He is and not just for what He does."

Prodigal Gatherings, the ministry founded by Tamara White, consists of a downtown Denver coffeehouse aimed at homeless teens, as well as their coffeehouse and club house in Aurora, Colorado, aimed at teens and children of families living in ratty motels, infested with crack, prostitution, and child molesters. The staff and volunteers of Prodigal play games, talk, take kids on outings, and hold Bible studies in an attempt to form relationships and create a ministry of Christ's presence among hurting youth.

Plans are under way to expand Prodigal to New York City.

"I could put one hundred volunteers and one hundred staff to work tomorrow," says Tamara.

Tamara lives in Denver with a nine-year-old child from her ministry that she hopes to adopt. She attended the Undergraduate School 1982–84, 1985–87.

14

FOR BETTER, FOR WORSE—I DO

• • •

THE STORY OF
AMY SWEEZEY WRENCH

OK, God, I thought You wanted me to marry this guy. What do I do now?

It was two days before our wedding. All our best friends were in town. The invitations were out; the church was reserved; we had the flowers, the photographer—everything was lined up.

Then my fiancé, John, came to me and said, "I've been drinking all along and hiding it from you."

It was forty-eight hours before the wedding I had dreamed of all my life. *What a time to find out my husband-to-be whom I thought was a* recovering *alcoholic had been drinking all along and hiding it from me!* I was so hurt. I was so confused. I was so torn.

The most difficult decision of my life was before me, and I couldn't figure out what to do. *OK, God can heal him; I should go ahead with the wedding. No, I cannot allow an alcoholic to be the father of my children. Maybe God is telling me not to marry him. But wait, God has brought us together. He wants us together.*

What am I supposed to do?

We immediately went in for counseling with our pastor to sort things out. I wanted him to tell me what to do, but, of course, he wouldn't. He said, "Amy, this is your decision. If you call off the wedding, I'll help you make phone calls and tell people it's off. If you want to go through with it, I will support you, love you, and marry you and John. This has got to be your decision with God."

He prayed with us and left the decision up to me.

My parents were in town by that point, and we spent a lot of intense time with them, trying to figure out what to do. My four bridesmaids, who were all wonderful Christian friends, prayed with me about what decision I should make.

Time rolled forward. The day of the rehearsal was upon us, and I still didn't know if there would be a wedding or not.

◆　　◆　　◆

John was not a Christian when I met him. He grew up in the Roman Catholic church, but he had never made his parents' religion his own. He just went to church as a child because that's what his family did.

After we met, he agreed to come with me to Kalamazoo Community Church for services. After attending, he said, "Wow, this is a totally different thing than what I've ever experienced before." God used this seeker-friendly church to break down the walls of "religion" that John had grown up behind. The people of this church loved God and loved one another. Because they were so relational, and because they were not caught up in appearances, John was drawn to the Gospel. The Holy Spirit used this Christian community and the pastor's message to prepare John for salvation.

One day, when John and I arrived at my parents' house for a visit, we sat in the car and talked. I explained how he could become a Christian, and he prayed to receive Christ right there in the driveway. What a joy to lead him to Christ!

But a salvation experience didn't mean that our lives would be problem free.

On our first date, we talked about alcohol. I don't remember how it came up, but he told me he didn't drink. I learned to hate drinking when I was growing up. Some of my relatives were alcoholics, and I saw how it devastated their lives and their families. So, on this first date, I asked John why he didn't drink. He gave many reasons, but he didn't mention that he was a recovering alcoholic.

I told him how I felt about alcohol, right from the beginning. However, the longer we dated, the more I found out about John's drinking problem. John had stopped drinking before we met. He admitted to me that he had needed to give up alcohol because it was starting to take over his life. Pieces of the puzzle were coming together and starting to make sense to me. His struggles were not unlike those of several of my relatives who were alcoholics.

I came to the point of accepting that he *was* an alcoholic, but there was no way I could be with him if he was going to drink. He was sober while we dated, but he secretly started drinking again while we were engaged.

At one point during our engagement, I found out he had been drinking. We had a big argument. At that point we were partway through our premarital counseling with our pastor. I said to John, "OK, this is it. Something has to change. Either you get your act together and stay sober, or I'm calling off the wedding. I can't marry you and then have children with you if you're going to be drinking."

In that counseling session with our pastor, John said, "I understand. I do have a problem. This is wrong and I'm going to stop." We prayed about it, and I really felt John was sincere and wanted to change.

We decided to move forward with the wedding. I thought we had this problem conquered.

But now, several months later, only two days before the wedding, we were back to square one, dealing with John's drinking problem.

What hurt me most was to discover that the only reason he told me about it this time was that some of our friends confronted him and said, "Look, John, we know what you're doing. We know you're hiding it from Amy. Either you tell her or we're going to."

Under that ultimatum he came and told me. *And he didn't even feel guilty.* I was so disappointed.

On the eve of our wedding, I was still wavering with my decision. *Should I marry John or call it off?* Preparations for the wedding kept rolling along. The planned wedding was getting closer each minute, and I was torn as to what to do.

At the rehearsal dinner that night, much to my surprise (and delight) John got up in front of everybody, including his family, and poured out his heart, admitting that he was an alcoholic. He said, "I have a problem and I'm not going to do it anymore. I'm going to go to AA. I'm going to get fixed. I'm going to ask God to help me." He did need help, regardless of whether I married him or not. But this was the first time he'd ever *gone public.* Before then, he hid it—never wanting his friends to know. He thought if they knew, then he would be held accountable and they wouldn't let him drink.

After hearing John admit he was an alcoholic, I knew

that he was ready to deal with the problem and take the steps to work through it. Our closest friends and family knew about it now, and that accountability and support was exactly what he needed. This was major progress, and that encouraged me.

If he was willing to do that, then I knew he was on the road to recovery. That gave me a real peace that God wanted me to go ahead and marry John. I knew it was going to be tough at times. I knew that we'd struggle. I knew that we'd have to get help through AA and Al-Anon. Whatever it took, we would find the help that John needed.

I decided to marry him.

Some people said, "Are you crazy? How could you do that? This guy is drinking and lying to you up until two days before your wedding. Just because he says he's sorry like he's done five hundred times before, why would you accept his apology? Why would you think he's going to change?"

But my parents and my godly friends who were closest to me all felt the same peace that I did. They agreed that I was doing the right thing.

We went through with the wedding, and it was the best day! I didn't have any misgivings or fears. I didn't have any *oh-no-I'm-marrying-the-wrong-person* moments. I really felt God in that place. The wedding and honeymoon were wonderful memories.

When we returned from our trip, John got connected with AA, as well as with some men in our church who wanted to help him get grounded in the Word. He knew if his Christian walk was to grow, he needed to be accountable to some other men.

I really believed that John was embracing sobriety and things would be different.

Everything seemed to be going great until nine months later. While I was out of town on a business trip, he drank. I didn't know about it until later. He continued drinking off and on for about a year and tried to hide it from me. I suspected it and questioned him about it, but he denied it. What was I supposed to do? Call him a liar?

I wanted to fix John. But it soon became apparent that I couldn't. I couldn't nag him into sobriety. I couldn't control him into recovery. I couldn't be with him every second of the day. I couldn't be lurking at every corner making sure he wasn't drinking. I couldn't be his conscience for him. His problem was bigger than all of my solutions.

At that point, I came to the end of myself. I let go.

OK, God, it's all You. I want to fix this and I can't; there's not a thing I can do about it. You can fix John better than I can, so I just have to let You do it.

I had to back off. I could not say to John, "Did you drink today?" I had to let God handle it and know that He was in control.

That was hard for me to do, because I was a controlling person. My tendency was to take back control from God. I often questioned what He was doing. I kept saying, "God, I understand that You are sovereign, that You know what You're doing. But why did You have me marry this guy if he was just going to lie to me, deceive me, and continue to drink?" I wanted to have kids with John, but there was no way that was going to happen with somebody who was drinking. I had seen too many lives in my family destroyed by alcoholism.

I have to admit there were times along the way that being out of control felt like free-falling. But I knew that when

I hit bottom there would be a soft landing, because God is faithful.

Every day I had to continue to struggle and remind myself that God's perfect plan was in process and gradually being worked out. God led me to John. I had to trust that He was working in my husband. I also realized that I had to "give thanks in all circumstances, for this is God's will for you in Christ Jesus" (1 Thessalonians 5:18 NIV). That wasn't easy, but through it all, I was becoming a more grateful and godly follower of Him. God felt very close to me. He was my lifeline. I don't know how people can deal with this kind of thing if they don't have God. If I didn't have God, I would have gone nuts!

This is why prayer is so important to me. When I was a student at Moody Bible Institute, my first roommate, Missy, gave me a blank journal book my freshman year. She told me to write down my prayers. It was the best gift I ever got in college, because it guided my prayer life. It allowed me to go back and realize, *Oh, yeah, I asked God for that,* and, *Oh, yeah, He answered that!* Keeping a journal helped me to see progress, to remember that God does hear and answer prayer.

One way God answered my prayers was by bringing the right people into my life at the right times. I never felt alone. Even though my struggles were difficult, I always felt supported and loved. As John and I have served in our church, helping with children's ministries, fund-raising, drama, and planning, we have felt the encouragement of a supportive Christian community.

This has been a great help to John as well. He never had any Christian friends growing up, and for him to be meeting with other Christian guys—praying, volunteering, and going to Promise Keepers—was such a cool thing. When he is accountable to someone with his prayer life, reading his

Bible, and focusing on his walk with Christ, then the drinking isn't an issue.

Our marriage is also about keeping God first. We pray together, and we read a devotional book together. When I'm down, he's up, and when he's down, I'm up. Like any other couple, we argue about socks on the floor and other things, but we know that we're in this for life, and divorce is not an option for us. We are going to do everything we can to safeguard our marriage.

◆   ◆   ◆

After John "came out" publicly and was sober for a while, we told our testimony at church. It was amazing the number of people who came up to us and said, "I was a drug addict for fourteen years," or, "We go to AA every week." The married couples that we thought were perfect Christians had their own addictions and things that they struggled with. We just never knew. Through the word of our testimony, our network of support became even bigger.

Our testimony has also given John opportunities to counsel one-on-one with other people who are going through addictions. Having been through all this has made us much more sensitive. This has helped us relate to others who are struggling, to show them love and share how God can help them.

A couple who are friends of ours were going through similar struggles, but they were not Christians at the time. Every day she was freaking out, calling me to talk about her husband's problem. It was driving her crazy. I listened empathetically, but it was also frustrating to realize, *She would be so much more at peace with this issue if she would just let God be in her life.* I could relate to her feeling of helplessness, but it was difficult watching her go through it without God. Through our friendship with this couple, they were able to see how John and I were dealing with addiction, and we'd like to think that our example helped bring them to God. Eventually they became Christians.

Although this testimony gave us opportunities to minister, it also brought grief. It gave some believers reason to analyze and judge us. Some people assumed we must be sinning. Why else would we have these problems? The Lord knows I examined my life over and over, agonizing whether all this was happening to me because I did something wrong. But I really *don't* believe that was true in this case. I believe with all my heart that God brought us together, and our love for each other can grow because of Christ and in spite of our weaknesses.

Alcoholism is a disease. It's not a matter of human willpower. When you're an addict, apart from the redemptive power of Christ, you are hooked. Alcoholism is also like any other sin. That happens to be the one in which John struggles. His sin is more outward and noticeable than mine. But I'm no better than he is. I cannot sit here and say, "He's the bad one and I'm the good one, because I'm not an alcoholic." People are labeled or looked down upon because they struggle with addictions like drugs, alcohol, or sexual sin. But everybody sins. The sins of some are more visible than those of others, but I'm just as fallen in my fleshly nature as John is. Jesus' blood covers all sin and provides forgiveness and grace to free us from its bondage. I pray that God will keep me from sin every day, just like John has to pray on a daily basis, asking for His strength to keep him from drinking.

◆   ◆   ◆

John has been sober now for more than three years. Yet I realize that a relapse is only one drink away. Satan knows our weaknesses. He is out to destroy us. We take that danger very seriously. But we also know that Christ gives us the strength and power to endure. Every day we pray that God will keep John sober. And that He will keep me supportive, to do whatever I can to keep us focused on God.

For better, for worse—I do.

◆   ◆   ◆

The Wrenches recently moved from Kalamazoo, Michigan, to Florida, where Amy is a meteorologist with Orlando's NBC affiliate, WESH, Channel 2. She forecasts the weather (usually sunshine) on the morning show, Sunrise. *She attended the Undergraduate School 1989–91.*

"YOU MUST LEAVE THE COUNTRY!"

◆   ◆   ◆

"You have one year to get out of our country."

The Colombian official wasn't joking. As an emissary for the president, he had the full authority to tell us to leave. We were being evicted. Our mission was being kicked out of Colombia.

The implications of his words could be devastating. *Decades of work washed away. Years of prayer and negotiation to win the right to enter the country. Thousands of hours of hacking through jungles, building airstrips, learning languages, building relationships, repairing airplanes, teaching agriculture, translating Scripture, and beginning to share the Gospel. Years of preparation by hundreds of people, now on the threshold of bearing fruit—all washed away.*

"I speak for the president. Your mission must leave Colombia."

I couldn't blame the president. The pressure was getting to him. His officials were constantly harassed by opponents who wanted to take over our linguistic and anthropological work.

"When are you going to kick the *gringos*[1] out of the country?" they asked.

To add to the pressure, our enemies "leaked" misinformation (translation: *lies*) about us to the press.[2] There was no telling what people might read about us in the newspaper. Rumor circulated that we were operating a uranium mine.

Though it seemed like a joke, people throughout Colombia were taking it seriously. People believed we had a hidden agenda. Instead of digging wells and teaching villagers how to get a better harvest, instead of learning cultures and languages, instead of operating a flying ambulance service, we were mining uranium from the lake at our center in Lomalinda. We were accused of flying uranium clandestinely at night to Washington, D.C., in our single-engine airplanes, where it was made into who knows what! *(Nuclear weapons, maybe.)*

Another rumor said that our fifteen-thousand-gallon water storage tanks at the top of the hills at Lomalinda were not cisterns, but instead were missile silos!

How could anybody believe this? I wondered. But one of our friends pointed to the reporter who was printing some of these stories. "Take this journalist seriously," he said. "He has deposed ministers from the president's cabinet by writing about them. Now he's on your case."

It became so bad that I was afraid to pick up the papers in the morning, wondering what new lies would be invented about us. Day after day, I went to the Psalms and found comfort from the words of David, who had also faced opposition and had been strengthened by the Lord.

The Lord gave us an answer and a strategy. We fought these lies with hospitality, openness, and transparent honesty. Now we needed to implement it with a new government administration. Again and again, we welcomed people of influence in the government and in the media to visit our center, learn about our operations, and find out the truth. As the director of our operations in Colombia, it was my job to handle challenges like this.

Cameron Townsend, the founder of SIL and Wycliffe Bible Translators, made a special trip from North Carolina to Colombia to help us repair relations with the Colombian government. Since the minister of education was closest to the president, "Uncle Cam" and I invited him and his family to visit our center and stay in my home. During his visit, he met with local politicians, all of whom gave us a glowing endorsement. He saw our work. When he finished looking around, he looked at me with a puzzled expression on his face.

"Where is this opposition coming from?" the minister of education wondered.

In the morning, my wife and I offered him breakfast. At the end of our meal, I spoke to our guests.

"We've had our physical bread," I told them. "Now it's time to share our spiritual bread, the Word of God." Then I turned to a Scripture passage and offered the Book to him so he could read aloud, since he was much more fluent than I was in his native tongue.

As he rose from the table he said, "Thank you for asking me to read the Scriptures. It has been a long time since I've done that."

Later he asked, "When will you next be in Bogotá? I want you to come to my office. I'll have something for you."

When we arrived in Bogotá, the minister of education thanked us again for being hospitable to him. Then he handed us a letter. That letter, which carried the president's implicit endorsement, was filled with praise for our work with the indigenous people groups.

"You may use this any way you wish," he said.

Uncle Cam looked at me after we left his office. "We need to make this public," he said.

We published the letter in the nation's three leading newspapers. Our public image began to change. But our enemies were not deterred. They kept looking for ways to get us removed. However, when the minister of the interior contacted university professors who were antagonistic to our work, he made an interesting discovery.

"We want SIL's linguistic files," the university professors said. "Since you're kicking them out of the country, pack up their files and send them out to our universities."

But the minister of the interior replied, "No. If you are going to take over their work, you are going to go out into the jungle and live with the people, just like the SIL people have been doing."

There weren't any takers.

◆   ◆   ◆

On another occasion, the vice minister of the interior said to me, "You're under investigation. We're investigating every mission agency in Colombia, because we're not sure what they're doing."

Again, the Lord directed us to be honest and open. I brought him a report of what our mission had accomplished during the previous four years.

He started paging through it, and then suddenly he stopped. "Whoa! This is really important," he said, as he noticed we had awarded more than a thousand diplomas in agricultural courses to Indian people during those four years.

Months later, I met with him again. He brought out my report and told me, "This is really important. You can't imagine how many times your opponents come here, sit in the same seat you're sitting in, lean over, and say to me, 'When are you going to get rid of the gringos?' I get out this report, and I turn to this page and show them that you awarded over a thousand diplomas to Indians in the last four years. Then I ask them, 'How many diplomas have you awarded?'

"They slink out of my office with their tails between their legs."

◆   ◆   ◆

We used the same open-door policy to deal with the journalist who reported that we were flying uranium and building missile silos. We picked him up and flew him in an SIL plane to Lomalinda. After a tour, he came to my office.

I was ready to field some tough questions, but he didn't give me any. "I have to apologize," he said to me. "I've been smearing your reputation without knowing the truth about your work. Today, I've seen it, and I assure you that my attitude is changing. When I go back, I'm going to write the truth."

He did exactly that. He visited several times to gather material, and he wrote a wonderful series of articles in the newspaper. On one of these visits, he brought his wife and his mother-in-law. They had a meal in our home. One of our Colombian employees, a new Christian, witnessed to the journalist's mother-in-law and led her to Christ!

This newspaper reporter, his wife, and his mother-in-law listened sympathetically to the Scriptures as we read them at the dining table. Shortly after that visit, he was killed in an automobile accident.

You never know when you may touch someone's life just before he steps into eternity.

◆   ◆   ◆

One Saturday morning, as I was starting to leave on an errand, a helicopter flew over and landed at our center.

I turned around and discovered that the helicopter was filled with top military and civilian officials, including two generals and a colonel. About that time a Colombian navy truck drove up with a crew of frogmen. The general asked if he could meet with my administrators and me. So his party went up to my office. We met around a big table, and he opened his sealed orders. He said, "We are here to investigate your work."

I said, "Our doors are open. Do what you want."

So he sent his signal corps to look over our radio communications and his air force people to check out our aviation program. An anthropologist reviewed our linguistics files.

The main party stayed through the morning. We prepared lunch for them. And then they conducted interrogations throughout the afternoon. The helicopter took off just in time to return to Bogotá before nightfall.

But they left a colonel in charge of intelligence to continue the investigation for another week, in case they'd missed anything.

During that week, our Colombian employee led him to faith.

Then the colonel left. So they assigned a captain to re-place him. And that man received the Lord. Finally, after three weeks they withdrew everyone. Perhaps we missed fur-ther opportunities to witness to the military!

Meanwhile, the frogmen were examining the lake. They were equipped with instruments to measure radioactivity. They stayed for ten days to see if the lake contained any uranium!

The captain of the navy frogmen celebrated his birthday during their stay. We invited them all over for a birthday party at our house. My wife, Margaret, baked a cake in the form of a Colombian ship; she even put a little Colombian flag on a toothpick. We entertained these men, and they be-came good friends.

When they left, the commander of the frogmen apolo-gized to me. He said, "You know, we have really bothered you people by having been here. I want to apologize and ex-plain that we were just following orders."

"No," I said. "We are happy that you came here so that you could check this whole thing out and give an accurate report back to your government."

He smiled. "You know, we only found one thing here."

That surprised me. "What did you find?" I asked.

He said, "The only thing we found was *la presencia de Dios*—the presence of God."

For me, that was a crowning moment of our ministry in Colombia.

◆   ◆   ◆

About this time, the journalist I mentioned was writing his series of articles. When I told him about this incident, he wrote an article in the newspaper called "La Presencia de Dios." As a result, the whole country learned that if you go to the mission center in Lomalinda, you will find the presence of God.

Some people will never experience the presence of God until they come into contact with you or me. Our work of translating the Bible in Colombia was centered on one purpose: to bring the presence of God to the people of that nation. Our enemies meant all of this opposition for evil, but just as He did for Joseph in Egypt, God turned it around for good (Genesis 50:20).

◆　　◆　　◆

In response to hard work by **Forrest Zander,** *Uncle Cam, and other members of the SIL staff, the Lord moved on the hearts of the Colombian officials, and the president issued a reprieve allowing SIL to stay in Colombia. In 1980, Forrest Zander was honored as Moody Bible Institute's Alumnus of the Year (Undergraduate School and Moody Aviation 1953–57). He now makes his home in Illinois, where he serves as Wycliffe Bible Translators' associate director of stewardship ministries and minister-at-large.*

BIBLIOGRAPHY

* * *

Chapter 1: Servant of Christ, Advocate for Equality
Mary McLeod Bethune

Crowell Library Archives. Moody Bible Institute, Chicago, Ill. Used with permission.

Francis, N. F. Letter written on behalf of Bethune-Cookman College, 1948. Used with permission from Moody Bible Institute, Chicago, Ill.

Herrick, G. F. "Loved, Feared and Followed," *Colliers* magazine (August 1950): 27.

Landrum, G. N. *Profiles of Black Success: Thirteen Creative Geniuses Who Changed the World.* "Historical Mentors of Black Success." Amherst, N.Y.: Prometheus, 1997. Copyright ©1997 by Gene N. Landrum. Reprinted with permission from the publisher.

Peare, C. O. *Mary McLeod Bethune.* New York: Vanguard, 1951. Reprinted with permission from the publisher.

Smith, S. *Who's Who in African American History.* Greenwich, Conn.: Brompton Books, 1994.

Chapter 11: May God Be Glorified . . . By Life or by Death
John and Betty Stam

English, E. S. *By Life and by Death: Excerpts and Lessons from the Diary of John C. Stam.* 2d ed. Grand Rapids: Zondervan, 1938. Reprinted with permission from the publisher.

Hanks, Geoffrey. *70 Great Christians: The Story of the Christian Church,* 2d ed. Ross-shire, Scotland: Christian Focus Publications, 1993. Used with permission from the author.

Hefley, J. C. *By Their Blood: Christian Martyrs of the Twentieth Century.* Milford, Mich.: Mott Media, 1979. Used with permission from the publisher.

Stam, E. A. *The Faith of Betty Scott Stam.* Philadelphia: Revell, 1938. Used with permission from the publisher.

Taylor, Mrs. Howard. *The Triumph of John and Betty Stam.* New and rev. ed. Philadelphia: China Inland Mission, 1935 (1982 Moody revised edition). Used with permission from the publisher.

Chapter 12: Praying Pioneer
George Verwer

Verwer, George. *No Turning Back.* London: Operation Mobilization Literature, 1983. Used with permission from the author.

NOTES

• • •

Chapter 1: Servant of Christ, Advocate for Equality
Mary McLeod Bethune

1. C. O. Peare, *Mary McLeod Bethune* (New York: Vanguard, 1951), 28.

2. Now known as Barber-Scotia College.

3. Peare, *Mary McLeod Bethune*, 63.

4. G. F. Herrick, "Loved, Feared and Followed," *Colliers*, August 1950: 27.

5. Peare, *Mary McLeod Bethune*, 67.

6. Nellie Francis letter, 20 April 1948, Crowell Library Archives, Moody Bible Institute.

7. Student Record, Crowell Library Archives.

8. Herrick, "Loved, Feared and Followed," 38.

9. S. Smith, *Who's Who in African American History* (Greenwich, Conn.: Brompton Books, 1994), 21.

10. Peare, *Mary McLeod Bethune*, 88.

11. Ibid., 95.

12. Ibid., 106.

13. G. N. Landrum, *Profiles of Black Success: Thirteen Creative Geniuses Who Changed the World.* "Historical Mentors of Black Success" (Amherst, N.Y.: Prometheus, 1997), 30.

Chapter 3: Love Speaks Every Language
Gary Chapman

1. Even though Karolyn was attending Tennessee Temple University, she had a similar experience of recognizing the logic of missions. By the time we married, we were both committed to a lifetime of missionary work.

2. At that time, Moody offered a three-year program. It now offers both four-year bachelor's degrees and graduate degree programs.

Chapter 8: My Grace Is Sufficient for You
Ian Leitch

1. As the formal entrance to the Moody Bible Institute campus, the Arch is a famous landmark among Moody students and alumni.

Chapter 11: May God Be Glorified . . . By Life or by Death
John and Betty Stam

1. E. S. English, *By Life and by Death: Excerpts and Lessons from the Diary of John C. Stam,* 2d ed. (Grand Rapids: Zondervan, 1938), ix.

2. Ibid., 20.

3. Mrs. Howard Taylor, *The Triumph of John and Betty Stam.* New and rev. ed. Philadelphia: China Inland Mission, 1935 (1982 Moody revised edition), 44–45.

4. E. A. Stam, *The Faith of Betty Scott Stam* (Philadelphia: Revell, 1938), 79. The hymn to which Betty was apparently writing additional verses was written by Clara H. Fiske Scott; it first appeared in Elisha A. Hoffman & Harold F. Sayles, *Best Hymns No. 2,* (Chicago: Evangelical Pub., 1895).

5. Stam, *Faith of Betty Scott Stam,* 113.

6. Taylor, *Triumph of John and Betty Stam,* 57.

7. English, *By Life and by Death,* 20.

8. J. C. Hefley, *By Their Blood: Christian Martyrs of the Twentieth Century.* 2nd ed., 1996 (Milford, Mich.: Mott Media, 1979, a division of Baker), 57–58.

9. Stam, *Faith of Betty Scott Stam,* 124.

10. Taylor, *Triumph of John and Betty Stam,* 91.

11. English, *By Life and by Death,* 46.

12. Taylor, *Triumph of John and Betty Stam,* 101.

13. Hefley, *By Their Blood,* 58.

14. English, *By Life and by Death,* 57.

15. Ibid., 61.

16. First expressed by Tertullian (A.D. 150–c. A.D. 225), see Geoffrey Hanks, *70 Great Christians: The Story of the Christian Church,* 2d ed. (Ross-shire, Scotland: Christian Focus, 1993), 21.

Chapter 12: Praying Pioneer
George Verwer

1. I finished in two years by transferring some credits and taking some courses by correspondence. I remember sitting in the bus station, supposedly on a date with Drena, working on correspondence courses.

2. I have since come to see that giving away everything for the sake of the Gospel can turn into a twisted and legalistic rule. Some, for example, feel it is unspiritual to maintain an attractive home. But I have found that a beautiful (though not extravagant) home can be a good witness to our neighbors of the joy we have in Jesus Christ.

3. George Verwer, *No Turning Back* (London: Operation Mobilization Literature, 1983), 70–71.

4. Ibid., 104.

Chapter 13: Offering Hope
Tamara White

1. God isn't afraid of our doubts. I don't think He even maligns our doubts. Our doubts, I think, can be a sign of faith. If you have never doubted, then could it be that your faith is doubtful? Although doubts may arise as our fallen nature tries to comprehend a sovereign God, doubts show us the boundaries of our faith—the places where God is giving us an opportunity to grow. Though my faith is stronger now than it was then, I still struggle at times.

Chapter 15: "You Must Leave the Country!"
Forrest Zander

1. North American foreigners.

2. The events described here took place over several years and illustrate the kind of high-level opposition SIL (Summer Institute of Linguistics, Wycliffe Bible Translators' sister scientific organization) faced in order to continue advancing the Gospel in Colombia.

S<small>INCE</small> 1894, Moody Publishers has been dedicated to equip and motivate people to advance the cause of Christ by publishing evangelical Christian literature and other media for all ages, around the world. Because we are a ministry of the Moody Bible Institute of Chicago, a portion of the proceeds from the sale of this book go to train the next generation of Christian leaders.

If we may serve you in any way in your spiritual journey toward understanding Christ and the Christian life, please contact us at www.moodypublishers.com.

"All Scripture is God-breathed and is useful for teaching, rebuking, correcting and training in righteousness, so that the man of God may be thoroughly equipped for every good work."
—2 T<small>IMOTHY</small> 3:16, 17

MOODY
PUBLISHERS
THE NAME YOU CAN TRUST®